THIS
CRUIS
LIFE

A COLLECTION OF AMUSING STORIES FROM THE POPULAR
YACHTING MONTHLY COLUMN

Libby Purves

THIS
CRUISING
LIFE

In association with

YACHTING
MONTHLY

ADLARD COLES NAUTICAL
London

CONTENTS

Published 2001 by Adlard Coles Nautical
an imprint of A & C Black (Publishers) Ltd
37 Soho Square, London W1D 3QZ
www.adlardcoles.com

ISBN 0-7136-6136-4

A CIP catalogue record for this book is available from
the British Library

The pieces in this book were published previously
in Yachting Monthly magazine.

Typeset in 10 on 12.5pt Garamond Light.
Printed and bound in Great Britain by the Cromwell Press,
Trowbridge, Wiltshire.

INTRODUCTION

I am, as the after-dinner speaker always says down at the YC, honoured to be asked. (By the way, if you ever have to give the after-dinner speech at a strange yacht club, the infallible way to your first laugh is to be rude about naval officers. Never fails. Don't know why.) My sense of awe and honouredness – rather like a spotty novice being given the wheel for 10 minutes – stems largely from the fact that it was *Yachting Monthly* which first took me to sea, some 20 years ago. At least, its small ads. And I am grateful still.

I was, you see, a late convert. In childhood I had only one experience, being taken out on the River Blyth in Suffolk by a hearty family friend in a small, disastrously tippy dinghy called the Argo. My friend's theory was that the presence of a small, stolid friend would somehow tranquillise her own nervy daughter. She was wrong. As we swung on to the wind, Harriet collapsed on the floorboards in a whimpering heap while I clung grimly to the uphill bit of the boat, scrabbling for a foothold. 'We're going to sink!' shrieked the child. 'Rubbish!' boomed the skipper. 'We're just clipping along nicely!' 'But you see,' wailed her daughter, in a phrase I have often remembered during arguments about whether it is time the kite came off, 'I don't like clipping along nicely!' No answer to that, really. Me, I went back to canoeing up the muddy creek to Dunwich.

But 10 years later came my road to Damascus. I was a student, working in a far-western Irish bar for the summer. One morning I met one of the previous night's drunks as I walked down to the pier to buy crab for the sandwiches. He asked me for a cup of coffee on board the 26ft Stella on which he was crew; I climbed down the ladder, stood in the cockpit and fell in love. I had never known it could be like this.

Beforehand, I associated all sailing craft with tippy, leaky uncertainties of the old Argo. But in this little boat, instead of a tangle of ropes-ends and discarded plimsolls, lay nothing less than a home. My eyes devoured the bunks, galley, varnished chart table and the oil lamp like Mr Toad eyeing up the canary-coloured cart. I saw the brass portholes and thought: 'I could look out and it could be Rio! Or Greenland! And I would have arrived, with just the wind!'

That was it. Before long I was leaving notes on the bar and running away aboard other boats. The next year I went as cook on an oyster-smack to St Kilda, spent a winter in Yachtmaster evening classes at Oxford (we used to go on the roof with a sextant and proudly work out that we were somewhere near Aberdeen), and then began the small ad blitz. I expressed willingness to 'cook, steer, scrub, haul, and sing' in return for 'tolerant skipper and serious sailing'.

It was perfect timing: inflation had just taken off, and people were taking the plunge and buying boats as never before, reasoning that the money would soon be worthless. Hundreds of owners who had hitherto relied on 'Good old Piggy' or 'Brian at work' to crew for them, were finding to their outrage that Piggy and Brian had become born-again Westerly owners in their own right. After weeding out the catamarans (snob, I was, in those days), the obvious loonies and any-one who sent a photo of himself instead of the boat, I still had dozens of genuine offers to choose from. For months I found myself, bag in hand, at the end of a different pontoon every Friday night. I sailed with some families, but more often with crews of men or single men of all ages. I learned a great deal: not least that the first act of a suspicious new skipper is to give you the helm and mutter 'follow the buoys out', before retiring below to press an anguished, bearded face to the porthole in case you hit one. They like to know as soon as possible what they have let themselves in for. I did not blame them: my own first enquiry was for a sight of the flares and liferaft.

That there might have been other dangers did not even occur to me. Maybe I was just thick, maybe we lived in a more innocent age (in 1973? Do me a favour). Maybe it was the explosion in cruising which destroyed a certain innocent confidence that a yachtsman is, by definition, a gentleman. However it was, I never seem to have considered that *Yachting Monthly* small ads would ever be answered by the likes of Jack the Ripper or Dr Hannibal Lecter. There were a few Mr Beans, mind you, and the occasional Major Gritpype-Thynne; but the hazards they presented were of the kind that any robust girl with a few evening classes behind her could surmount.

Sometimes I was even helpful ('Perhaps it's leaking because that brass thingy under the sink has fallen off?'). Sometimes I got a bit worried about how helpful I had to be ('Um – I'm not sure you can fend a boat off the side of the lock by standing on the deck pulling the shrouds – perhaps if we pushed the wall instead?'). But I did not drown, and had immense fun and crossed the Atlantic in the end. And I have kept some of the skippers as friends to this day.

Does anybody do it now? Or has the pusillanimous fear of strangers, the scourge of our nervy society, spread to yachting? Would you, Madam, leave Newhaven on a strange man's Itchen Ferry without checking anything more intimate about him than his bobstay? I think we need a social survey on this.

Don't Plan

Yachting is full of contradictions in terms. Every other thing we mention is an oxymoron made solid, like 'cruiser-racer'. Or 'gourmet boil-in-the-bag dinner'. But of all the weaselly phrases, the king must be 'cruise planning'. Face it: if you've planned that closely, you aren't cruising. You're achieving. Conquering fate. In other words, working. Of course, maybe that is what you want to do. A disturbing number of cruising yachtsmen seem to have become infected with a John Ridgway-style determination to pit themselves against the odds, test themselves to destruction, and generally drive their families crazy. You can see them in harbours on dubious drizzly mornings, jumping up and down in the cockpit barking, 'Warps, Jamie! Tessa, never mind the laundry – leave it in the bags – if we're off the bar at 0840, down at the Head by ten, we still have to keep up 6.4 knots, which is going to mean the spinnaker right from the harbour mouth.'

You can also see the unlovely sneer on his wife's face; and upon his children's the grim, set look of offspring who are planning to jump ship forever as soon as they turn sixteen.

Yes, yes: we all commit ourselves to a prompt departure occasionally, when there is a deadline on a bar, or a vital tidal gate to hit. Just as we all motor-sail, under the same occasional duress. But just looking at this chap – the knotted veins in his forehead, the expression of anguished urgency – you know that he does this every single day of the holiday. That he will never be content to ghost along at 1½ knots, and that he takes it as a personal insult every time the ship and crew fail to meet their schedule.

You will see him again, sitting in the August sunshine in Dartmouth with clouds fluttering gaily past the castle and his children contentedly splashing, and he is not smiling. Oh, no. Say 'Nice day!' to him as you row past and he will howl confidingly, 'We're supposed to be in Salcombe. Hang-up with the engine. Got three hours to make up tomorrow now, it's a damn nuisance.' You know that he got the charts out from under the spare-room mattress back in December and has been hard at it with the calendar and the tide-tables ever since. You know that he had programed 198 way-points into his GPS by 31 March. You also know that he is doomed to perpetual disappointment. This man has a tragic flaw: he is a compulsive Cruise Planner.

The only hope is that he might be new to sailing, and that within a few years he will have been beaten down by Fate, wind and Sod's law just like the rest of us. We all used to Cruise Plan, in the beginning. There was the year Paul and I first met, as colleagues in the Radio 4 *Today* office. He had a Plan to deliver his Jaguar 22 from Burnham-on-Crouch to Portsmouth. Every Monday the whole office used to wait with bated breath (and smothered giggles) for his report. He would stump in and collapse in a chair while we all gathered round. 'Well,' the bravest would say. 'Where did you get to?'

It was a breezy southwesterly summer and for several weeks the answer remained 'Burnham. I went back. The mooring's paid for anyway.' On one breathless occasion he got as far as the South Foreland, and was driven back to Ramsgate. The next Monday we were all pretty excited, expecting any amount of southing and westing, but he just snarled 'Lowestoft' and went silent. Headwinds can do dreadful things to seasick chaps in pocket cruisers.

We then got a Contessa 26, and instantly began making great Cruise Plans to get to the west of Ireland. We always made it to Fastnet, but then usually fell foul of the mysterious great tide which sweeps yachtsmen into Sonny Sullivan's bar in Crookhaven and pens them in there for days, singing.

Once we got as far as Valentia, and on another occasion Smerwick; the Cruise Plan all the time being Inishvickillane in the Blaskets. We used to pin up postcards of it in the winter, but have never been there yet.

Gradually, we got humbler. When we sailed round mainland Britain, a journey quite often completed in a fortnight; we allowed four months. Even so, large numbers of intended harbours – such as Kirkwall and Hartlepool – hurtled past us on the tide, unattainable. On the other hand, Wells-next-the-Sea was delightful, though we had never even heard of it until the last-minute queasy scrabble through the pilot book.

The more we sail the less well-planned our cruises get. We now go along with Frank Cowper, who wrote the first real yachtsman's pilot, *Sailing Tours*, between 1892 and 1895, and opined that a certain innocence was essential in cruising, 'As the rash mouse, contemplating the tasty cheese, ignore the dangers surrounding it'. Start first, he advised, and read about the dangers when you get a bit closer. Have a pilot and charts for everywhere you *don't* mean to go (well, this side of Rio), and never repine at having carried useless ones. Never, ever, write your destination in the log until you get there (or, if you must, use the naval expression 'passage towards').

We once set out from Tréguier towards Alderney and reached

Dartmouth 26 hours later. And no, we were not lost; it was just the most comfortable course to sail. Like Chesterton's drunkard on the rolling English road, we are always pleased enough to get anywhere safely, be it Birmingham or Beachy Head:

God pardon us, nor harden us;
we did not see so clear
The night we went to Bannockburn,
by way of Brighton Pier.

Baby Blues

One thing they never tell you at the ante-natal classes is that all this huffing and heaving will result in your boat sailing away without you. They ought at least to teach you some special deep breathing exercises to do at the terrible moment, some months after the mere biological birth, when another umbilical cord is cut – or at least uncleated – and you push your little craft away from the mother pontoon without you. Because Mummy has to stay and look after the offspring, while Daddy does the big delivery trip to your next cruising ground.

We never really intended that this should happen. Babies? Hah!

chuck 'em in the pipecot and take 'em to sea! We had read a lot of gung-ho books about sailing couples who took their litters gaily round the Horn; we thought we could do it as well as anyone, being joint-owners of the boat, joint-skippers, each as keen as the other.

But when one of us turned into a Mummy, everything changed. We did take the children sailing, even at appallingly young ages which we now flinch to remember. But practicality soon crept in, and we came to accept two things. First, that although children can do any passage once they have got their sea-legs, those long early-season delivery trips are no fun either for them, or with them. Secondly, that we are not ruthless enough to leave them ashore and risk ourselves both at once through the shipping lanes. Result, one land-bound, sullen Mummy, and a Daddy rather smirkingly volunteering to 'do us all a favour' and make the big deliveries with a friend.

Now a boat, after a while, becomes a pretty intimate thing for a girl. Having your brand-new genoa torn by some over-enthusiastic winch-gorilla is as painful as having him tread on the hem of your new ballgown.

Grateful though you are to your husband and his hunky crew, the combined effect of intense jealousy (they always get marvellous weather) and the discovery of alien, septic socks under your personal bunk-cushions can bring on severe post-delivery depression.

Besides, on every trip Paul claims to learn some arcane new art of seamanship which I cannot match. Once (after I had fallen down the concrete steps of the Penzance aquarium and broken a bone in my ankle) he had to deliver our boat to Cork. He picked up, courtesy of the then Penzance Harbourmaster, Martin Tregoning, a smart young merchant officer who spent the entire trip trying to teach him how to work out spherical triangles for sun-sights using the Decca as a calculator. It was months before I could get him to admit that the page of thirty-five spidery calculations left by his new friend was, in fact, as opaque to him as it is to me.

Many of the delivery trips have been with Tom. Tom has a large family and a consequent willingness to run away to sea whenever asked. In the summer months the two of them start having furtive telephone conversations, parts of which are relayed to me. 'Well – we thought Cherbourg, but Tom wants to go to St Malo because he was once in prison there, just for the night, and he'd like to see the old place again . . .' or 'It might be better if we went all the way round to Brest, save you and the children the Chenal du Four . . . he knows a bar in Brest . . .'

Glumly, Mother packs the coolbox for her wandering boys (who follow a strict 1,000 calorie-an-hour diet while at sea) and waits for news.

News is not always prompt. One year, they took our old boat across to Holland in a westerly Force 7. Knowing exactly how fast she usually went, even under storm jib alone, I expected word from them the next morning. Silence. I rang IJmuiden, where I was assured by prim Customs officers that (a) no such boat had been cleared, and that (b) it would be quite impossible for anyone to enter the canal system without their knowing. I rang Den Helder. And Scheveningen. Same answer. By mid-morning it became clear to me that wherever they were, it had to be land. Possibly an offshore bank. The weather worsened. I continued to exchange hypocritically cheery telephone conversations with Tom's wife, and businesslike ones with the Coastguard. ('If you're quite sure they actually left, Madam . . . you'd be surprised how many of them turn up in Walton Backwaters fast asleep.')

At 1500, Paul rang. From Amsterdam. 'Oh, we just steamed through IJmuiden in the rain, nobody seemed to notice. We did think of calling you on the VHF, but we were busy making a bacon sandwich.' After the earful he then got, he has made it his business to 'phone me from everywhere, especially since we got the cellphone. One time, he rang from the River Ore Bar at 0800 as I was orchestrating a school run. He informed me that the engine had failed and the wind dropped, leaving them anchored a couple of metres from the sand with a fast ebb pulling them on. What did I suggest?

They are off to Dinard any day now. Me, I am taking the 'phone off the hook. As Tilman said, every herring must hang by its own tail.

More Blessed to Give

You can call me old-fashioned, but I do believe that plastic scrimshaw should only be exchanged between consenting adults. Likewise drinks coasters with knots embedded in them, miniature brass cannon, and absolutely anything with a brigantine etched on it. A consenting adult, in this context, is someone who has been heard to say, loud and clear, 'Gee! Amazing how hard it is to tell that reproduction scrimshaw from the real whalebone carvings! I couldn't half do with a cigarette-box in that stuff!' or who already owns, and prizes, a substantial number of olde naval rum-tot measures and desk paperweight compasses in low-maintenance varnished brass. It helps if his lavatory paper is known to emerge from beneath a small model of a unicycling sea-captain.

Otherwise, for heaven's sake give the man a bottle of Scotch. For yachtsmen, and women, December is a most perilous time of the year: when their non-sailing friends or relations pick up one of half-a-dozen nautical mail order catalogues and stick a pin in something shippy. Come Boxing Day, large numbers of us will therefore be staring gloomily at Cutty Sark plates, fridge magnets in the shape of lifeboatmen, Lord Nelson-type repro blazer buttons and – festooned with twiddly bits and already leaking paraffin – 'historic' lamps that never were on land or sea.

It is not that we are ungrateful; far from it. It is just that none of these artefacts is going to be of the slightest use in (a) making us dream happily about our boat in winter, (b) retrieving said boat from a disgusting fungal miasma during the spring, or (c) sailing it in summer. Yet it would only have taken a slight change of emphasis to make us really happy. To find under the tree, perhaps, a lovely big agricultural plastic bucket *with a rope lanyard already properly spliced on it*; or a spare roll for the barograph; or a box of new 3B pencils. Or a tin of anti-fouling. Or (oh, you shouldn't have, darling) a hand-held GPS with a pretty ribbon on it. For that, we would overlook the windjammer wrapping.

Oh, all right. It really is too much to expect people to wrap up smoke flares and fresh sink-filters. Even at wedding present time, most guests look at the list and understandably jib at putting their name down for the plastic toilet-brush and holder, or the washing-up bowl. Presents are symbolic, as well as practical, and Auntie Mary may feel squeamish about putting a new set of Lavac valves into one of her famous quilled-paper gift boxes.

However, there still remain presents which are romantic yet relevant. Most sailors are hideously superstitious, and would not sniff at one year's star gimmick in the RNLI catalogue, the keyring artfully fashioned from the prop of RMS *Queen Mary*, and guaranteed to have crossed the Atlantic 1,002 times (OK, it did it underwater, but it got there). That year RNLI was also selling a rather fine cloth parrot on a perch, highly suitable for giving to red-hot boy racers who own virtually nothing not made of carbon-fibre, and squeeze out half the tube of toothpaste on Friday nights to save weight for'ard.

One of the best presents we ever had in the romantic, winter-dreams category, was a ship's bell with the new boat's name engraved on it. We keep it, naturally, hanging on board to be tinged

by bored children. Equally distinguished was
the moment when a great voyager
gave us a visitors' book which had
already been round the world,
empty, as his own spare. Best
practical present was a new
boathook, from a chap who must
have watched us trying to pick
up buoys with the old one. Worst
intra-marital present was a plastic
solar shower device guaranteed
to drench the unwary with still-icy
water and get tangled up with the
warps in the cockpit locker. Best
was a barograph, which has
enabled us ever since to sit by the
fire in the autumn months, sucking in
our teeth and shaking our heads with
the sage observation that we were
right, that Low was deepening far too
fast for us to have missed the Thomsons' party and delivered the
boat back round the Foreland in the dripping rain.

Probably the most inspired presents you can give to cruising
families, however, are things which pack small and keep people
happy for hours of enforced inactivity. Happier, anyway, than a set
of collectable sailmakers' thimbles would have done. With a flash of
genius, the RNLI has had in it's catalogue not only the LCD pocket
computer Bible (Old and New Testaments at the push of a button, a
text for every disaster), but one of those jigsaw holders which enable
junior members of the family to start a huge puzzle when galebound
in Fishguard, pack it up instantly when the wind moderates, and
resume in Porth Dinllaen a day later. A boon to anyone who has
been thwarted in attempts to set sail by having to search the bilge
for Nelson's missing nose.

Still, there are all sorts of motives for giving presents. I have my
eye on a diabolical little special offer headed LOG YOUR ENGINE
HOURS: a display that switches on and starts counting whenever the
engine starts. Perfect for the yacht club swank who pretends he
'never uses the old iron top'sl except to get into the berth'. He'll
never let anybody below decks again.

The Scrooge Guide to Boat Shows

Any day now, Earls Court exhibition centre will start to pump out that heady smell that drives me wild. Aaah . . . resin, rope, tarred twine, onions from the hot-dog stand, damp raincoats, and new flax canvas, neoprene valves and a faint ghost of engine-oil . . . yes, yes, I could easily become a Bilgex-sniffer. A chandlerholic. The very thought makes me grope blindly for my credit card. All reason is suspended in the dazzle of GRP, the blink of brass and the seductive winking of liquid-crystal longitude displays.

Which, of course, is the whole idea. The January Boat Show is perfectly placed on the cusp of the year, far enough from last season's bitterness for optimism to have flowered again. Besides, it does not do to think too much about one's actual, real-life laid-up boat at this time of year. Far pleasanter to take your mind off the sinister mushrooms and green patches under the winter cover with a bit of restless waving of the Visa card. Buying treats for a boat, I always find, is much easier than actually looking after it.

But this time I have come as Ebenezer Scrooge. Ever since certain wild spending sprees some years back we have been practising continence. You need to psych yourself up for this mental discipline well before the Boat Show, so let us begin now: the knack is very simple. All you have to do is, whenever a tempting item has you twitching towards the plastic, take a deep breath, look again, and *imagine the worst*. Stop, for one moment, thinking about how nice it will be when it is spewing out weather maps, fixing your position or hauling up your anchor. Think instead how much you would *hate* it when it betrayed you. Conjure up that boiling resentment, that desire to smash an axe through its expensive innards, coupled with the frustrating realisation that if you do so you will invalidate the guarantee. Think of yourself bucking the tide through the Needles or queasily eating a bacon sandwich at 0300 off Noss Head, and imagine that – perhaps through no fault of its own, a power failure maybe, or a pulled-out screw – your expensive new mistress has let you down.

I speak as one who covered miles, on foot, trying to order a replacement part for a folding yacht-bike acquired at a long ago Boat Show in order to save me walking. I also speak as the wife of one who ruined two perfectly good cruises in our old Contessa by installing a 'bargain miracle' battery-state indicator with winking lights. It was supposed to wink red, green, or amber. In no time the salt air made it begin flashing like a fruit machine trying to forecast Three Mile Island. The devilish bit was that it would work for a day or two, to lull us, and only then go critical. Paul must have accumulated hours of sea-time with his bum sticking up from the engine compartment as he shouted 'Red – red and green – yellow flashing – GREEN AND RED AND YELLOW! £18.90 I paid for that thing!' And we shall not even mention the patent roller-reefing line winch which nearly broke my wrist so many times that we finally donated its safer components to the children's model Thomas the Tank Engine in the garden. Nor the shopping-trolley with some daft name like 'Marina Pal' which filled the hanging locker with flakes of rust in the few brief weeks before its wheels fell off.

Feel cooler, more judgmental, more cautious? Good. Such miserable reflections have probably eliminated the frivolous impulse to buy. If it is a genuinely useful item, you might still buy it, but you have faced the worst. *Tout lasse, tout passe, tout casse*, as the French say: the slickest plastic casing gets a crazed and sullen look after two seasons; the niftiest GPS might get trodden on in a moment of high emotion, the most respectable manufacturers sometimes nod off on the job. Step forward the leading (very leading) British manufacturer who sold us a log-and-echo-sounder combo at Earls Court some years ago. It worked for two seasons; since when we have paid more in winter repairs than it cost in the first place, and it has messed us up season after season. We have cruised hundreds of miles with a trailing log, leadline, and gritted teeth, while this damn thing's cockpit repeaters stared mockingly at us. Eventually the echo sounder problem was solved, but the log stubbornly refused to read, despite two winters with the manufacturer and an acrimonious conversation with their service department in which some oily swine said, 'Look, love, when we mend things they stay mended.' Finally, they admitted the origin of the problem: a super new American component in the repaired impeller unit which ensured – wait for it, wait for it – that it works perfectly as *long as you keep it bone dry*. Hence its clean workshop record every winter, and its underwater betrayal of us every summer.

I am not saying that nothing ever works or that nothing is ever worth it. Plenty of things truly change your life for the better. All I am suggesting is that if you feel poor this year, you can save yourself a lot of money by having the baleful daydreams, as well as the rosy ones.

In the Bleak Midwinter

February is for me a landlocked month: the farthest away from sailing both in fact and in spirit. The brief happy hysteria of Earls Court is over, the boat and her various dinghies are slumbering mouldily under their sagging winter covers. Even the pipe-dreamer of the family has momentarily stopped making wild, mad plans to circumnavigate Scandinavia or spend an invigorating summer dodging pack-ice in Scoresby Sound. Something about the note of the wind which rattles the windows discourages fantasy: it will take the first daffodil, the first southerly breeze, the first shedding of the thermal vest to remind us that we meant to repaint the cockpit this year and send the sails for service.

It was not always like this. Before family life crept up on us, we quite often used to brave the winter seas. Paul has vivid, not to say hallucinatory, memories of a particular passage he made alone from Ramsgate to Rye in a Jaguar 22 with the kind of cockpit designed for sinking rum-punches in the Florida sun, not cowering in February sleet. He finally made it in a flurry of snow; entering Rye, however, his mouth was so frozen up he couldn't answer the Harbourmaster's enquiry as to where he came from. 'Ramsh – Ramsh– eheu, koff, koff,' was as far as he could get.

Around the same time I was optimistic enough to enrol for a sailing course in early March: we crossed the Irish Sea, holed up in Waterford for two days, shuddering, then came back with a Force 8 behind us and a sinister areola of freezing fog around each navigation light. I have never been more grateful to be fat: the two slenderer members of my watch went into that curious, sub-hypothermic doo-lally mental state. They stared into the night and said things like 'Lighthouse? Yes, light. White light, right. Flashing. One, two, five, six, four. Is it morning?' As duty navigator I decided around 0300 that their observations could perhaps not be completely relied on, and stayed up myself to look out for the Smalls light.

But as we grow older and softer, and are blessed with the wonderful excuse of children, we tend to stick to Sealink and Stena for the winter months. We did go through a phase of attempting, in a pathetic, woolly-gloved manner, various maintenance jobs which would have taken half the time and effort in April. Sometimes it was quite enjoyable, particularly the bit where you go into the misted-up

marina cafe and have egg, bacon, beans, sausage, chips and a fried slice, cramming the vital calories into your mouth with tar-stained hands and fingernails full of sandpaper. But we got cured of that long ago, at Bradwell, and have not done any really cold-weather work on any boat since.

It began because, when our first child was due, a November baby, we panicked and changed up to a bigger boat the preceding summer. From our neat, perfect little Contessa 26 (which would have held one baby easily), we promoted ourselves to a rather old, heavily foxed Rustler 31, fitted out in an era when Formica was king, and which, while solid, roomy and well-equipped, had all the interior charm of a transport caff somewhere on the A1, *circa* 1962. This offended our nesting instinct, and Paul took to fleeing London in order to spend every available weekend on board, transforming the pilot bunk into a massive padded cradle, fitting neat bits of varnished mahogany moulding around each bleak grey-white surface, and screwing brass lamps to the repulsive old quilted headlining.

It never quite worked. We reached possibly the nadir of this maintenance programme on the February day when I bravely agreed to bring the baby, Nicholas, down to Bradwell Marina for his first visit to inspect the boat's new look. We were going, at the time, through a lot of heart-searching about whether, with this vast new responsibility, we would ever get to sea again. We wanted some sign, absurdly, that the baby would take to sailing.

It never rose above zero; at midday we could still see our breath on the air; the heater didn't work. I sat huddled up with the baby wrapped like a Russian babushka in a multicoloured cot blanket, saying, 'Yes, very nice, it looks t-t-t-terrific.' Never has a boat seemed so comfortless. The baby stared, and sucked, and stared again, apparently horrified at this new life we were preparing for him. I hummed the *Mingulay Boat Song* to try to inspire him. Paul said, 'Right, never mind, we'll get a cup of tea down us,' and lit the fearful paraffin stove (bought in preference to gas, for the baby's greater safety). It flared, and died, and refused to hiss again, however well-pumped. Cursing, Paul began to take it to pieces while I and the baby sat and tried to look nonchalant and pleased, and the sleet fell on the cabin roof.

After 1½ hours and the complete dismantling of two burners, he got enough action out of the stove to boil a kettle and make us a cup of tea. We drank it, locked up in the last of the light, and drove rather silently back to London. 'Oh, you went to the boat,' said friends. 'Lovely. Did you get much done?' 'We made a cup of tea,' we snarled, and walked stiffly indoors.

On Being Pretty

There is a lot to be said for being pretty. Not personally – hell, I wouldn't know – but nautically. If you are shopping for a boat take a tip from me: opt for the one which looks as if she could have been an illustration on a birthday card. Think classic, think gaff and topsail, bowsprit and baggywrinkle. Never mind if an equivalent in modern design is more practical, cheaper, roomier, sails faster and spares you the ridicule of being caught trying to hoist your jackyard tops'l upside-down at an OGA rally. It is all worth it. The more classic-looking your boat, the more people will – against all reason – be nice to you.

I have sailed on several boats which make onlookers reach for their cameras. There was *Kathleen*, a Brightlingsea oyster-smack with proper flax canvas sails (atrocious on the knuckles, but their faded shades of tan drove amateur watercolourists wild from Pin Mill to Portree). There was *Sheltie*, a 19ft Itchen Ferry whose bucket lavatory and devilish folding chart table were a constant torture to her crew, and whose low profile ensured bootfuls of water in anything over Force 2, but whose cutter rig drew 'Aaaahs!' all across Lyme Bay. There were various interludes on Norfolk wherries, Brixham trawlers, and ancient canvas-topped narrowboats. Then there was *Grace*

O'Malley, a Cornish Crabbers' pilot cutter; and although my brother never missed an opportunity to murmur the old seafaring saw 'Nothing be naffer than a plastic gaffer', her laid decks disguised her GRP identity sufficiently for us to have wasted many a roll of the public's Ektachrome in the years we were together.

Admittedly, there are drawbacks to being on a photogenic boat. You live in dread of collision, because tripper-boats (and not a few small merchant ships) make a point of coming as close as possible to take pictures of your cute brown sails. You never know they have seen you, until you spot the telltale camcorder poking over the bows. At which point the wash hits you, and sends your darling old-fashioned gaff crashing across in a genuine, authentic Chinese gybe.

But on the whole, there is nothing but advantage in being pretty in an obvious, nostalgic way. Long observation as a crew makes me conclude that both Harbourmasters and fellow yachtsmen forgive you for duff manoeuvres far more readily on a traditional boat. They take your warps, and initiate conversations in a way they do not for a glistening Moody or a stout practical bilge-keeler with a top on it like a butter-dish. And sometimes, wonderful things happen.

We were making along the Normandy coast one July, and by mere chance sought shelter not in Fécamp, but the little locked harbour of St-Valéry-en-Caux to the east of it. After a long night sail from Cherbourg, we were just having that ratty conversation – you know, 'Is that the entrance? My God, look at the tide off that buoy – no, seriously, I think we should get the main off now – it'll be even windier under the cliff – oh, all right, do it your way – children, shut up.' As, purple in the face, I wrapped myself around the gaff and its flogging sail, an inflatable dinghy shot out of the harbour mouth. 'Vous êtes ici pour la fête?' 'Quelle fête?' 'La fête des vieux gréements.'

Ever since Brest 92, French harbours a hundredth of the size have been crazy to organise their own classic rallies. 'Mais,' I cried fluent-ly, 'On est plastique.' 'Ça ne fait rien,' cried our host gaily, and explained, over the flogging sails and the growl of his outboard, that if we lined up in the basin with the other boats and decorated our-selves we would be honoured guests of the town, moored free, fed dinner and breakfast and invited, what is more, to a *vin d'honneur* with M le Maire. 'On y est,' I cried triumphantly, and in we slid, among the dozen-odd genuine veteran craft.

We had no flags with which to dress overall, so we begged the string from the local chandler's ceiling. We slung a hammock and stationed children in it to look sailorlike when the public came by.

I have to admit that the rest of the weekend passed in a bit of a haze. There was the time in the marquee when I found myself leaning on a Dutchman, being conducted by the deputy Mayor in a shanty about health to the King of France and *merde* aux Anglais. There was a surreal conversation with a ten-year-old child crew on the home-made galleon *Avos* from St Petersburg, bound for Vietnam and handing out leaflets saying 'The private company Gladkov & Sons is an independent organisation aimed at the reconstruction of the Russian fleet, the building and exploitation of small and large ancient sailors and teaching Russian people navigation'. They were there by accident, too. There was the bagpiper brought by the RNR, marine bands and shanties all day, a naval battle, fireworks and an outdoor Mass for sailors, with our startled children enticed into carrying banners in the procession round the harbour.

Of course, it would still have been fun if we had just gone to watch, in a gaffless, sensible, state-of-the-art modern boat. But not quite *such* fun.

Dinghy Molesting

Everyone with a secret vice knows when they are at their most vulnerable. As part of my therapy I would like to share with you the fact that in spring I come into my most dangerous period of the year. My keepers have noticed, with a sinking heart, all the early spring symptoms of addiction: I am seen stuffing secret brochures into drawers when my husband approaches, and caught half-way through surreptitious 'phone calls to obscure businesses in seaside towns.

Unfortunately, there is no helpline yet for my condition. Perhaps as a result of this brave confession, someone will set one up: Dinghyholics Anonymous. And for my spouse, SKODA: Support for Kinfolk of Dinghy-Dependent Adults.

For I am a slave to dinghies. Can't resist them. In choosing and buying yachts I am quite sensible and responsible: I listen to surveyors and take advice. But dinghies are different, because they are just within the range of a card-assisted impulse buy. And there is something about them that seduces me. Rubber or canvas, folding or wheelable, carvel or clinker, pram or pointy: I just find them gorgeously irresistible. My heart beats at the sight of their glistening showroom shapes, their artful new features, perky little oars and strokable varnished thwarts. Dinghies! All fresh and clean with their bright brass rowlocks and perhaps a darling little folding-up mast and adorable lugsail! I want them all.

At Boat Shows, the pushers know me well: half-excited, half-apprehensive, they semaphore from JM Henshaw to the Barrow Boat stand as I reel between them groping for my credit card and being restrained with difficulty by an anxious family. I am the Humbert Humbert of the tender world: no glassfibre coracle, no disastrous Heath Robinson folding device with forty-seven hinges and a mysterious canvas flap, is safe from my predatory attentions. I kept the *Yachting Monthly* surveys on folding dinghies and sailing tenders for two whole years in my wallet, just to gloat over in secret, on the train.

Sometimes I get my wicked way. In spring Paul lives in dread of the Roadline lorry and the fatal words, 'Could you give me a hand with it?' He knows that the only thing which needs two men to lift it off a lorry has to be yet another super lightweight, easy-launch, all-purpose wonder dinghy sold to his wife at the Boat Show three months ago, in some stolen moment while he, poor devil, took the children to the loo.

They will, I tell myself, all come in handy. But the shaming fact is that aboard *Grace O'Malley* what we actually use is a plain elephant-grey British Yachtsman's bog-standard inflatable, whose make I need not even mention. You know the one. It is not pretty, but rolls up small and does the job. When ours got stolen and I was despatched to the Boat Show on my honour not to buy anything but an exact replacement, I reluctantly kept the faith: my only lapse being to add a hundred quid's worth of ingenious folding floorboards which then jammed up the stern locker.

Meanwhile, the home dinghy fleet expands, and occasionally, when money gets tight, contracts again as I sell on to a fellow dinghyholic. The veteran of the current fleet is the small ancient Tinker Tramp, which sails questionably and does not fit our present deck layout, but which I have managed to foist on my younger brother on a long loan. Paul thinks I have sold it (ha ha!) but I have not. It is still mine, all mine, even if it does live in Southampton. So is the world's-cheapest-yellow-dinghy, known as HMS *Bumwetter*, which with fiendish cunning I pretend is the children's. It travels just aft of the mast, getting in the way, and gives everyone a thorough soaking annually.

Then there is the folder. We shall not speak about the folder. It threw me into the cold Irish Atlantic three times before I finally saw the light. It is still on the market, a snip. Then there is the glassfibre number, the holes in its keel interestingly full of shingle, which dates from the time I used to grow a crop of noxious riverweed under a Drascombe Dabber on a mooring. The shingle-keeled craft usually stays afloat for just long enough to reach the mooring, so I lend it to my other brother (I have a third brother in reserve, next time Paul insists I pretend to sell one). But it is still part of my proud fleet. As are the daughter's scruffy Optimist and the son's antique Mirror with genuine centreboard jacuzzi effect. Oh, and the Wanderer which succeeded the Dabber, and in which I try to convince the family they would love to come for picnics.

But my best friend of all is the sailing inflatable Star Traveller, one of the first they made. In this I ricochet my rubbery way from buoy to buoy, secure in the intimate knowledge that only I truly understand it, especially since the slow leak in the port tube. On the wind, you have to kneel up as if on a crouching version of the Windsurfer, and support the mast by hooking the port shroud round your shoulder. Off the wind, the soft tube makes a comfortable bed, on which I frequently fall asleep in light winds, to be woken by a squelching collision with the bank.

Paul heard me talking to the makers at the Boat Show about its resale value, and felt a surge of hope. Poor fool. The truth is that the latest model looked so tempting, with its jolly yellow tubes and dinky new shroud tensioners . . .

I feel a Roadline lorry coming on.

Early Worms

It is a curious business, writing about cruising – one so rarely has the chance to write while actually on a boat. All sorts of things impede onboard literary labour: the rusting qualities of typewriters (second only to those of folding bicycles), the way power adaptors for high-tech laptops go missing and the battery is flat anyway, the dispiriting fact that the ink from Biros always leaks into your knicker bag and dyes your bum purple, and the navigator's dog-in-the-manger attitude to pencils.

One is also impeded from writing while afloat by the debilitating effects of fresh air, whisky, and the insidiously comforting thought that no editor knows how to get hold of you anyway. But never mind that. The point is that yachting journalists, with a few hardy and well organised exceptions, write while ashore. This leads to

several distortions of reality.
The first is a tendency
to get suspiciously lyrical
about the suck of the tide,
the light on the water, etc.
The second is a reaction
against this, in which you
become heartily practical
and focus on the most
obvious things: safe boats,
navigation, food, comfort,
speed, harbours, all that
stuff. The third is an
attack of Ancient Mariner
disease, causing the writer
to relate some bygone
and largely imaginary
personal adventure at sea
involving the Portland Race,

the ultimate gale, homicidal bulk carriers, a daring rescue and a
near-death experience with a killer dolphin trained by the CIA to
loose poisonous darts.

To all of these distortions I plead guilty. So one summer I took a
notebook to sea in order to capture the true priorities. Unfortunately,
such is my handwriting that I cannot make out most of it (What can
'bedbug riot' mean? And what is that bloodsmudged word beginning
with an F, next to 'split-pin'?). But at one stage I seem to have seized
the indelible felt marker we keep for re-marking the rubber dinghy,
and written in sprawling deranged capitals, right across one page,
the words: GETTING THE BASTARDS GOING IN THE MORNING!

This, it would appear, was more important than food, stowage,
harness design, mooring fees, GPS, or any other aspect of cruising.
Reading that shaky script I remembered everything in a red mist of
renewed aggravation, and understood the secret of harmonious sailing
with friends or companions. *Getting them going in the morning* is
the key.

Or, conversely, if you are the other party, being able to get some
peaceful sleep at nine o'clock in the morning without some ragingly
impatient woman banging around the boat, loudly dropping winch
handles on the deck above your bunk. In other words, before you
ever ship with anybody again, let alone marry it, make absolutely
sure that there is harmony between your circadian rhythms. Your

body-clocks. Otherwise precious hours aboard will be spent with one of you yawning and the other nagging.

My own history, as the mad scrawl indicates, is that of a woman who loves sailing first thing, watching the cows on the shore wading in mist, the clear pale early light touching the mountaintops, the fishing boats plunging seaward, all that. My idea of a really good start to the coasting day is shivering out of the bunk at 0530, downing a mug of tea, catching the tide round the headland and dropping the hook in shelter for a bacon sandwich. We have achieved this a few times, but not often; I married a man who reckons that the whole point of being on holiday is to lie in your bunk till after 0900. We begot children who entirely agree with him; even the one who does wake naturally prefers to devote the first three hours of her waking day to lying under a duvet reading *Jill has Two Ponies*.

While they do this, I take down the shipping forecast, read Patrick O'Brian for half an hour, then get up, noisily stuff my sleeping bag into its daytime stowage, push back the hatch with a loud scraping sound, peer out, say, 'Aaah! Northwesterly, couldn't be better!', clatter the kettle, let it boil until it whistles deafeningly a foot from their heads, make tea, switch on the radio, and clump about on deck exchanging loud pleasantries with nearby boats.

None of this has the slightest effect. They moan and pull the covers over their heads. Outside, the tide flows past, wasted, and the early sunshine fades to grey drizzle. (Have you noticed how often, in British summers, the best weather happens between 0500 and 0900?) By the time they manage to prop themselves more or less vertically and peer out, the world looks so unappetising that they flop back for another hour. Alternatively, in tropical latitudes they decide that it has now got so hot that it would be unsafe to sail until the noon heat has passed, and go back to sleep anyway.

I do not know what to do about this. You can, of course, put out to sea without getting the sluggards up. One disadvantage of this is that they wake up feeling sick. People lurching greenly from their sleeping bags to start the day draped over the lee rail are not ideal companions. The other disadvantage is that whatever happens leaving harbour – you know, scrapes on the quay, collisions, mooring lines round the propeller, assaults by unexpected sandbanks, the usual routine sort of thing – will be entirely your fault, and the slugs will emerge from their beds of idleness straight on to the moral high ground, saying, 'If you'd just waited 10 minutes while I dressed . . .' as if there had ever been any possibility of that happening within the hour.

No: there is nothing for it but to endure. And, of course, to ruin their convivial evenings by unrolling your own sleeping bag at 2100 in the saloon and insisting that your circadian rhythm, too, is sacred.

The Ferry Home

There are some experiences only Channel and North Sea yachties share. Not just the obvious ones: fighting the Portland Race; untangling a spinnaker-wrap while travelling sideways past the Needles on a 4-knot tide; dodging super-ferries in the separation zone; or haggling with your lovable marina management about whether it is really fair to include the thickness of the stick-on letters on the stern to your chargeable LOA. These may be the things we prefer to talk about at the club bar, but we bear other secret scars in common. Since this piece is the nearest you are likely to get to a therapeutic forum for yachtsmen, I feel we should air these private griefs occasionally.

My theme is the 'ferry home' syndrome. You know all about the 'ferry home'. It may look like an ordinary floating duty-free shop, full of more or less contented landlubbers clinking back to Blighty with nothing more depressing on their minds than the M3. But to a certain damp brotherhood with canvas trousers and bagfuls of grubby clothing, these ferries are transports of the damned. They

represent defeat, aborted cruises, miscalculations, and shivering dawns listening to the shipping forecast and realising that – even though you did cavalierly spend the last few francs last night – you are not going to see Poole again this side of the approaching Atlantic front. Time has run out on you.

So you are going to put the sailcovers back on, change more money, give the marina office another week's worth, buy a fresh Telecarte, queue for the 'phone box, negotiate a foothold on the next ferry and re-think the rest of the season. No wonder you look so sulky by the time you get on the soulless great deck: seatless, cabinless, ragged and unshaven, you stand out a mile from the carefree holidaymakers around you. Not least because you spend the whole journey leaning over the rail to check that the sea really is as rough and wild as the Met Office said it would be. For the final prickle in your crown of thorns comes when it blows a moderate, sunny Force 4 all the way.

This happened to us once, when we had waited two days for a break in the weather in dreary IJmuiden dock, run out of holiday, tied up the boat in an upstream marina, and taken an expensive and complicated overland journey to the Hook and the ferry home. By the time the weather finally changed for the better we were committed. All the way across, gentle breezes played through our hair and little yachts bobbed happily past. At least the year when we jumped ship at St-Valéry-en-Caux to come ignominiously home on the Newhaven ferry, you couldn't stand upright on the deck without holding on. That was a great comfort.

Sometimes, of course, the 'ferry home' has been resorted to for other reasons than bad weather. If it is planned, things are not so bad. We left Cherbourg one spring as part of a careful boat-delivery scheme, and only suffered the minor inconvenience – familiar to foot passengers in an age when ferry companies only care about motorists – of having to wait an hour and a half like cattle in a bus on the quay. But with us was another family, back from their own attempt at a week's foreign cruise, and like the Ancient Mariner they told us their story. The yard had launched them two days late; they dashed to Jersey, made for Cherbourg but got the propeller round a bit of cordage so solid that it succeeded in bending their rope-cutter. They limped in, had the boat hauled out and cleared, and set off again, only to be met by terrible tin-can sounds from the prop as it mashed into the cutter. So they got hauled out again . . . well, you get the picture. Having run out of time, there they were with the rest of us cattle on the sweltering P&O bus.

That was the classic 'ferry home' situation: nothing to look forward to, frustration to look back on, and the romantic mastery of your own ship suddenly snatched from you and replaced by ignominious pedestrian status. But yawning in the comfortless surroundings of Portsmouth railway station at 0630 after that trip, I remembered another variation on the theme and felt a strange nostalgia.

When you are young and broke, you crew for older and richer skippers. So you sometimes find yourself racing wetly across the Channel, and having to leave the ruling classes to their leisurely long weekend on Deauville racecourse and their cruise home on Tuesday. This entails spending an uneasy night on the ferry home with the rest of the young and poor. Hence the memory that hit me. Some time in the mid-1970s, I found myself on Portsmouth station at 0600, in company with three squaddies who had crewed the army boat in the race. They were trying to get back to their Midlands barracks for the first parade; I was trying to get to Oxford for a 0900 shift on local radio. We used the same achingly slow patchwork of milk-trains.

And the happy memory, since you ask, is that between us, by the time we passed Didcot at 0833, we had entirely finished my bottle of duty-free *ordinaire*, Rod's bottle of rosé, Eddie's champagne, and Dave's half-litre of Famous Grouse. If you're still sailing, lads, and you read this, I do hope the parade went OK. My day at work is best forgotten. Blame the 'ferry home' syndrome: another unsung part of the great yachting experience.

Cooking with Gas

Forget Communism and Capitalism, Mr Darcy and Mr Wickham, York and Lancaster, Tom and Jerry. Forget all feuds in life and fiction: for sheer intransigent stubbornness none can match the heartfelt, the accusatory, the passionate dispute between yachtsmen over the question of Gas versus Paraffin.

We stumbled into this row quite by chance. Back in the naive old days, we had a Contessa 26 with a gas bottle mounted (horrors!) *underneath the stove*, right down there in the heart of the cabin. We turned it off at the bottle after every single cup of tea, mind you, and sprayed the top periodically with tell-tale foam; but there it was.

I got a little bit thoughtful after seeing a Twister burn to the waterline in Glandore Harbour, and the gas explosion scene in

Bernard Cornwell's yachting thriller *Wildtrack* did not help much either. But by that time we had a Rustler with an inherited paraffin stove and felt smug about our safety from explosion and our terrific blue water credibility. In those days, the theory was that you could get paraffin more easily than gas in your average Third World palm-fringed island, so ownership of a paraffin stove carried a certain cachet. It was assumed that you were off any minute to wilder shores. We glossed over the fact that the evidence of our increased personal safety was two sets of permanently singed fingers and a doubled incidence of seasickness owing to the smell. We were, briefly, paraffin prigs.

Grace O'Malley, however, was designed with a draining gas locker, so with secret relief we capitulated. The way the gas pipe crept through a sealed locker under the children's bunks upset me a bit, so we put in an alarm and had many a merry nocturnal session trying to turn its false alarms off.

Eventually, we settled for a rigorous routine of tap-turning, and a flame failure device, which meant that after lighting the gas you had to stand there pressing the knob for what felt like half an hour before it would 'take'. But we thought no more of paraffin.

Fate, however, brought it back into our lives. Our Rummer yawl came with a paraffin stove. Taking her over mid-season, we resolved to re-learn its harsh disciplines. There was a wee pressure problem at first, which resulted in Paul's first attempt at a cup of tea sending a curtain of flame from stove to deckhead as the dribbled paraffin ignited. This being Falmouth, luckily, we were able to call in the great Jeremy Burnett, formerly of West Country Chandlers, and request some intensive paraffin-stress counselling. His sage advice resulted in hours of fiddling with the tank, and the unauthorised removal of the tongue from my spare pair of deck shoes 'to make a sort of gasket'.

It worked for a while, but every time Father said, 'Right, cup of tea I think,' the two children would move silently to their self-appointed posts, one standing by with the dry powder extinguisher and the other with the fire blanket unfolded and ready for action.

During the Falmouth Classics we were almost seduced into keeping the damn thing forever. The Rippingill Romantics are very persuasive: they gave us all sorts of cunning tips about special pre-heating jelly or nasty little jars with adapted Tilley Lamp fuses soaking in meths to replace our foul plastic funnel arrangement. They told us of gas explosions they had known, and stressed that on the Rua'ha-Oh'au archipelago, or 150 miles up the Congo, we would

look pretty silly asking for Camping-Gaz. They stood there on the moral high ground with their brown crispy fingers and their folksy breakers of paraffin lashed with obscure knots to the sternrail, and we almost gave in.

But not quite. For one thing, we found out that one of the most passionate paraffin men, who made light of our difficulties in getting the damn thing going in a seaway, is allegedly in the habit of lighting his stove at the beginning of a cruise and never letting it out. His ways, we decided, were not ours. Also, a lot of paraffin fans seemed to know nothing of modern gas stoves with flame failure devices; they implied with hauteur that the choice lies between a superbly engineered paraffin stove and some tinpot caravan rubbish using gas. Which is not quite the case.

So we are ditching it. *One stove and tank, slightly foxed, incorporating portion of historic deck shoe, seeks good home.* However, the dire warnings against gas have taken effect. We have instructed the boatyard to build on deck, just for'ard of the doghouse, a structure we call the 'gas-house'. It will hold one modest Gaz bottle (the spare being stowed on the sterndeck under a fetching canvas hat). It will have ventilation louvres everywhere, and the pipe-run down through the deck will be barely a metre long, its whole length clearly visible and squirtable with leak-detector, with a tap at the deckhead. It is the ultimate neurotic bit of installation.

And nobody need ever know. Robertson's of Woodbridge are skilled wooden boatbuilders, adept at pastiche; we have requested them to make this little varnished gas-house strong enough to stand on or brace against, and above all to look as if it has always been there. As if, perhaps, it has some virtuously shippy function connected with the storage of tarred twine or the mounting of a pelorus. We may get away with keeping our shameful secret at the next Classics. Especially if we take care to singe our fingers and smell powerfully of meths.

Test Schemst

There is a wonderful man called Ted Osborn whose mission it is to write the *Newswatch* column in the Cruising Association's quarterly bulletin. This unsung hero trawls through the dullest, the most turgid, the most opaque legislation at home and abroad in order to feed CA members with memorable little nuggets and bits of advance warning. Like the possibility that you might need to be a registered childminder before you take your small children's schoolfriends fishing; or that it emerged in Parliamentary Questions that the 1750 LW shipping forecast can be delayed if it clashes with the infernal Test Match.

But for one bulletin he found a corker, a lulu, an unforgettable threat hanging over us all. It is about Belgian legislators this time. 'New regulations proposed', he said in that deadpan way of his, 'include a stringent fitness test, written test and practical exam applying to any person navigating a pleasure craft within . . .' – wait for it, wait for it – '50nm of the Belgian Coast'.

Pause, to listen for the sound of well-upholstered bodies thumping to the floor in East Coast yacht clubs. The grandiose 50nm limit proposed by the barking Belgians is bad enough. A few minutes with chart and dividers over the breakfast table demonstrated just what bad news this is for the pedalos at Margate or anyone on a Li-lo off Broadstairs beach, and the very dubious legal status of windsurfers at Felixstowe. Channel crossings to anywhere east of Boulogne clearly become impossible, the Straits of Dover impassable by those whose Walloon was not quite up to Question 27a, and the slightest touch of imprudent leeway on passage from Burnham-on-Crouch to Ramsgate in an offshore breeze could lead to boarding by the Belgian Fitness Police who patrol the 50nm limit tirelessly. Look out for international incidents.

Oh, all right, we may laugh. Obviously someone is gently going to point out to the Belgian imperialist tendency that 50nm is a bit ambitious. But what struck me especially, was the fact that, aside from knowledge and practical testing, the framers of this measure have added 'a stringent fitness test'. Which is, of course, yet another example of the fatal confusion of yachting with sport.

Would Long John Silver pass, or the prosthetically challenged Cap'n Hook? Or Nelson? Would our friend X, who weighs upward of 20 stone and is famed for keeping going all night while thinner men fade? Would Hilaire Belloc, who was too fat to get into a bunk and had a special platform on the floor, surrounded by bottles? Would my other friend Y, who is colour-blind and just back from Spain (made a change from the usual North Norway run)? Would the old boy we met in Fowey one year, who gracefully declined an invitation to drinks because 'one does tend to fall out of the dinghy after a drink, these days'? He was off to the Isles of Scilly to pick up a 'young chap' of eighty-one. Come to that, would my fellow-columnist Mike Richey, who was shipwrecked in his mid-70s and has had a new *Jester* built since, in which he has worn even more grooves in the Atlantic?

Actually, Mike might pass; but it would hardly matter if he didn't. It takes a Belgian bureaucrat to make a connection between a skipper's ability to do 100 press-ups and his or her competence to be out on the sea. Yachting – except at the tiresomely sporty end, with which we brass-lamp sailors need not concern ourselves – has very little need for sports fitness. A skipper requires intelligence, sea sense, ratlike cunning and a good dash of cowardice (all right, prudence). The latter qualities will ensure that the boat that skipper sails is physically within his or her limits: better spend a couple of days ashore fitting easy and disaster-proof reefing tackle than doing abdominal crunches and hammering the pec-deck.

Better a spreading bum and a touch of rheumatism earned by days and years of canny survival on the water, than a magnificent physique and a handful of certificates. In my small-ad sailing days, I was always fascinated by what happened in the night on cruiser races. You would have this boatful of hunky, magnificent gorillas of the tanned rugby coach-type, muscles gleaming and moving like racehorses. They would spring around with spinnaker poles at the start and draw my girlish eye.

Ignored by me, there would also generally be a thin, hollow-chested weed with pebble glasses and a stutter, called Raymond or Nigel, who did not seem to fit in. You assumed he was the skipper's boss, or brother-in-law. But by midnight in a nasty head sea, the rugby coaches underwent a transformation into pumpkins and lay useless below, groaning and shivering. Nigel and I would go round wrapping them in blankets, then sail the boat for the rest of the night. We would be watched, from his command-bunk, by the skipper. He rarely got up, being usually a bit dilapidated himself (from working hard enough in an office to pay for the damn boat in the first place, have the Belgians thought of that?). But he knew the sort of people a boat needs to get it safely from A to B.

And in those days, we did not live in terror of a task force from Zeebrugge raiding Ramsgate Harbour with sphygymanomometers and portable ECGs.

Hot Dreams

Before we start on the rambling chronicle of another year's cruising, I suppose I had better tell you the disgraceful story of how, in the cold months of one particular year, I seduced a good man away from his principles. Ready?

The man in question was my husband, Paul. He thought, poor sap, that by marrying a girl he had rarely seen without a woolly hat, he would be forever safe from the Delilah blandishments of sunstruck women.

He had seen only too often what happened to hardy northern-waters sailors like himself, never happier than when shuddering over a pot of cocoa in Scapa Flow. They got married, and were inexorably lured south by their womenfolk until they became pathetic figures pottering around Majorca in motor-sailers with naff awnings. This, he felt, must never happen to him.

He nurses a high and noble belief that the winter months of a Proper Sailor were intended by God to be spent heavily clad, upside-down in the drizzle with a scraper. Luxury, to him, was having a dry rag of towel to put round his neck at the start of a watch.

I, however, had a stiff shoulder. The physio said winter sun would do it good. So I told him we were going to the British Virgin Islands for a week in February, to taste hot-weather sailing.

'Never!' he cried nobly, not unlike the boy on the burning deck. 'February is for sanding down the cabin doors I brought home, and buying new Lavac valves! February is for sorting the charts out in numerical order and writing in all the Notices to Mariners about oil-rig movements!' I insisted. I said he would like sailing in the

Caribbean, honestly: not so different from the West of Ireland, only warmer, and with coral instead of just rocks.

Sullenly, he packed a woollen bobble-hat. All the way to the airport I could see him thinking: *This is not the way to do it. If you are going to the West Indies what you do is haul round Ushant, thrash down to the Canaries, and spend a month rolling violently down the trades worrying about the keelbolts.*

I slightly agreed with him, having once sailed from Gran Canaria to Barbados and felt like Columbus for a whole year afterwards: but nonetheless held firm. A week was not long enough to sail there; so we would cheat, and fly.

When we got to Virgin Gorda and the Bitter End Yacht Club's white strand, he was a bit mollified by the fact that there were clouds. White, puffy, trade wind clouds. One of his major complaints against the Med when we did a flotilla there was that it was overlit. The skies were too blandly, boringly blue; there were no interesting cloud shadows to watch. This was definitely better. But you could see him thinking, *Too fine to last, there'll be a depression through tonight, could be fog . . .*

The Bitter End boasts a 'yacht club atmosphere'. Paul was pretty puzzled that anyone should actually use such a claim as an enticement. Our wide acquaintance with yacht club atmospheres at home, gleaned on voyages round Britain, suggests that they are not complete without a harassed lady frying chips in sump-oil, the odour of the hot fat mingling with that of mouldering oilskins and (in older clubs) decaying leather armchairs; also a coven of mumbling old men peering through the fogged window at some hated enemy making a mess of picking up his mooring, and a spotty lad behind the bar hitting a beer barrel hopelessly with a hammer.

However, it turned out that they meant an *American* yacht club atmosphere, which is more what we would call country-club. Pretty damn nice, anyway.

So we sailed and pottered in the Sound aboard dinghies, Rhodes 19 keelboats, sailboards, Boston Whalers, Sunfish and kayaks. And then out to sea, on a Freedom 30. By this time I knew he had undergone some profound, corrupting change because he had bought himself a baseball cap.

The real shock, though, came when we sailed the Freedom 30 with its lotus-eatingly easy rig and self-tacking headsail. It had never occurred to him, in a stern life of staysails and topsails and bowsprits, that you could tack through a narrow channel in a Force 6 without sending your family scuttling round two sets of headsail winches every time. And, moreover, without wearing a shirt. He started to get a dreamy, faraway look.

Once, as he rubbed sun-oil in his palms, I could see he was missing his winter maintenance programme, but the moment passed. He looked around sometimes at the boats in the anchorage, enjoying the occasional 'Psha!' at some particularly naff piece of Caribbean gin-palace engineering; but then other boats, strong, beautiful creatures from Maine, would take his eye and he would drum his fingers and say 'We could do the circle, bring the boat out here one winter, then follow the sun up the East Coast . . .'

This is a breakthrough. Normally, he goes on and on about the Lofoten Islands and how to reinforce the hull against bergy bits. I could feel, day by day, the crumbling of his lifetime's resolve to stay cold and stern and Northern.

When we got home, he went to a chandler, as real men do in winter, and came home with a packet. I looked inside when he wasn't around. He had bought a windscoop! This could be the beginning of a whole new direction in our cruising. You wouldn't buy a windscoop to go to Lerwick, would you now? It goes to show: give a man a lotus, and he'll eat it.

The Uses of Men

Extraordinary, the way time behaves at sea. We have often spent several hours in a nasty tide-rip only to discover that it was, in fact, 20 minutes; and on other occasions lived through a whole crowded season's worth of incidents and alarms in the course of four days.

It happened again on a fitting-out cruise in South Brittany. Between Monday and Friday morning we experienced three appalling anchorages with all-night rolling, an episode on legs to avoid same, a rope round the prop, a graze of razor-sharp rocks, a spot of involuntary mountaineering, midge-bites, snorkelling, sunburn and seasickness. We had to get a day-cabin on the ferry back to sleep it off, and got positively nasty with people who said 'feeling nice and fresh after your break, then?'

We did, however, do rather well at getting assistance; which means that, to my satisfaction, I won a couple of skirmishes in the permanent, wordless battle which exists between many spouses over the matter of soliciting help. Most men, probably because of some dark testosterone-driven compulsion to blaze their own trail through

life, detest asking for help. Just watch them in a strange town, accelerating grimly past any pedestrian whose benign, settled aspect might tempt their wife to wind down a window and ask the way to Empire Crescent. Recent research into gender and conversation suggests that this is not actually male arrogance but male insecurity: they are convinced the passer-by will lie to them, exploit them or rob them, whereas women are trustful. Maybe. The sure thing is that the masculine approach slows the journey down no end.

On yachts, there is an even stronger determination to be self-sufficient at all times. They take their cue from Tilman's remark that 'every herring should hang by its own tail', and those stalwart pioneers of sole Atlantic races who refused to take radios because, if unlucky, a chap should hazard no rescuers but 'drown like a gentleman'. Not that most men would take it quite that far, certainly not with families aboard; but the desire for sturdy independence colours every decision (help from satellites, strangely, seems not to count).

We women, on the other hand (once we are past the chippy teenage-feminist stage), believe in using every available source of advice and assistance. That, boat next door, includes you.

My husband being actually very competent, I have to admit that my triumphs have been few. I do have a certain pathetic way of standing on the bow approaching a berth which quite often gets our lines taken by kindly passers-by. Before GPS I once sneakily got a position off a passing coaster in the middle of a nasty North Sea passage while my husband slept, and on another occasion, borrowed a shackle key from the boat next to us in a marina to save getting out the pliers. On all these occasions our benefactors have been only too happy to help: because, interestingly, while men hate asking for help they absolutely adore giving it (indeed, I can hear myself getting like my old Granny, who used to say complacently 'People adore doing little things for me, dear'). The fact is that everyone likes helping: we have seldom had such a buzz as when we rescued the marina master from Amble Harbour when he fell off the pontoon, and then even rescued his hat; or took letters ashore for one of the old manned lightships. It gives you a secret, lifeboatmanlike glow.

Anyway, to return to the fitting-out cruise. The first crisis was the entanglement in Le Palais inner harbour. Our propeller is deep and hard to reach, and the tide was dropping under us, and we had taken off the legs. Off-season, I scoured the sleepy little town for a diver. Amazingly, I found one who happened to be painting the bottom of the dive-boat, and who had his gear with him by accident. He got down to it, and with some difficulty freed us; accepting only a cup of coffee and a modest tip.

So on we sailed to the narrow fjord of Ster Wenn, where the pilot book brags of 'rings set into the rock' for your stern line, since there is no room to swing and two anchors would be asking for trouble. We searched vainly for rings, then noticed a French boat full of fit young men, with its stern line looped round an inaccessible-looking crag way above the jumbled low-tide rocks. I made my usual disgraceful suggestion. Frost. For a while, we tried swinging. The rocks got closer astern. The wind freshened. Dusk approached.

In the end, I rowed up to the French boat and hinted the unspeakable. Could we, er, bend our line on to theirs just to bring us clear of the rocks? Delighted, they sprang into action, despatching a lad to swarm up the rocks with our own line. You could tell it made their day, rescuing *les maudits Anglais.* So we were all happy. Except Paul, who still wants to know exactly what I said to the French skipper.

He got his revenge. They left before us in the morning, so I had to climb up and untie the damn thing myself. Amazingly, after a night's sleep it turned out not to be that bad. We could have managed, hung by our own tail.

But I prefer it my way – although be warned. Speaking as a short-handed, harassed, exhausted cruising mother, I have to tell you that when I see a boatload of fit young men just sitting around, I regard it in the same light as a marsh full of delicious samphire, or a harbour tap, or a fair wind: just another God-given resource to be exploited.

Sail with a Purpose

I have a confession to make. I think I have done too much cruising lately.

I use the word 'cruising' in a fine-tuned sense. We have in this family – ever since it was a family, ie a small quarrelsome unit containing children – made a very clear distinction in our sailing between the 'delivery' and the 'cruise'.

The delivery is the bit where you get the boat to somewhere nice. You try to do this without anybody on board who is puking into a potty, lying sullenly in their bunk with a Walkman, or uttering the unspeakable words 'Are we nearly there?' just as the wind hardens and settles cosily on the nose. The delivery is something to be got over as fast as possible; often outside the timespan formally designated as 'holiday'.

The cruise, on the other hand, is a matter of daysails and nights in harbour – or perhaps occasional short, exciting, starry nights with dawn arrivals for a big cooked breakfast in a new port. It is a time when you decide where to go each day depending on wind and whim. The art of the cruise lies as much in finding good beaches close to the anchorage as it does in seamanship. It is a holiday. Children love it. All is harmony (well, nearly all). Maybe the cruise ends on a bit of a delivery – say Cherbourg to Poole, something to make everyone aboard feel like Columbus – but nothing drastic. Certainly not Ushant to Ipswich in one leg.

At the beginning of our family years we did not recognise this distinction.

Didn't want to: I think, subconsciously, we knew that once you dislocated pleasure from purposefulness in sailing, it was the beginning of the end. So we hammered 1,700 miles round Britain with children of three and five, and for the next two years cavalierly loaded them aboard at places like Swansea Dock and belted off towards the Fastnet before anybody had got their sea-legs.

But at last we capitulated and a system grew up wherein the delivery was, by tacit consent, an adult business. In this way we have managed as a family to cruise the entire coast of Normandy, Brittany down to Quiberon, and the far west of Ireland. But the deliveries – Woodbridge to Brest, Dartmouth to Kinsale, that sort of thing – have been undertaken by my husband and a motley selection of male companions, because somehow we could not bring ourselves to vanish out to sea together, a father and mother of small worried children. And this is how it is that I came to do too much cruising: not in itself, but too much proportionate to delivery.

I went soft. From being someone who would happily beat to St Kilda, I became, as a mother, the kind of strategist who could set out for Alderney and end up in Dartmouth because the wind was more comfortable that way. From being someone who thought nothing of spending three consecutive nights at sea two-handed, I caught the infantile, short-hop habit of thinking 14 hours a long day.

And indeed, it is. All days at sea are long if you expect a harbour by suppertime. You don't eat properly because you will later; you don't catnap because you expect a full night's sleep; you keep glancing at the GPS to see how far is left to run. You become discontented, focusing more on the land than on the voyage to be made towards it. Or, if you spend only short drifting days and hours on beaches, you feel a deeper discontent. The boat we owned then, *Grace O'Malley*, was a great strong creature, more than a caravan. She was made for voyages. It took me three or four years to put my finger on what was starting to be wrong with sailing for me; the penny took a long time to drop.

When we finally sold *Grace* we needed to bring her home from the Quiberon peninsula, 240 miles round three fast tidal headlands and across the Western Channel to Falmouth, in three days, with time only to anchor against tides. And, the children being older, we did this deed together and without them for the first time in 13 years.

It was *wonderful*. We had light headwinds and rough seas, a blocked fuel pipe in the Raz de Sein, strong headwinds in the Channel, and Paul threw up incessantly in the ship's bucket, almost drowning the radio during Mr Major's epic resignation speech in the

Downing Street rose garden. But we were buoyed up by the sheer exhilaration of only having ourselves and the boat to think about. And above all, in a way I had quite forgotten, by the satisfaction of doing a delivery: a necessary passage to a stated end. It gave the trip dignity. We were a mailship, a tea clipper, an East Indiaman hurrying home. We had a goal. We almost (but not quite) understood why people with limited time go racing, just for the sake of being given a task and having to complete it.

And now I feel ready to cruise again. See you up the Helford River, with a picnic.

Power Woman

Anyone who has been hanging around boats for 20 years or so, especially older boats, will know what I mean by Elderly Petrol Engine Syndrome. EPES is a mental ailment caused by early contact with *certain engines*. It grips thousands of us, blighting our boating and causing grey hairs, stammering, anxiety and irritable skipper syndrome. The symptoms are a complete inability to trust any engine, ever.

You can spot an EPES sufferer from the other side of the harbour. Whatever the boat, however modern and well-maintained, he or she will, under no circumstances, leave the berth, or arrive at one, with the sail-covers and ties on. If the boat is under way, even from one berth to another one 50ft away, the EPES victim will have ensured that all the sails are ready for hoisting, and will probably have laid out huge sweeps on the sidedeck, ready in case the wind drops. Not to mention the boathook, the anchor, and a full set of fenders.

He, or she, will then bend to the ignition key, switch on, and listen to the contented, even chugging of the engine with head cocked and a satirical expression. As if to say, 'Hah! It's pretending to be working. That's what it wants you to think!'

Captain EPES will then ease the boat into gear, grimacing horribly, and express the same mistrustful amazement when it actually goes. The sufferer's face will not unpucker itself until the sails are up and the engine – treacherous, scheming bastard! – is switched off.

The whole performance is watched with amazement by younger, or luckier, yachtsmen and women who have been brought up with reliable, kindly marine diesels which never miss a stroke. They put it down to mere paranoia or senility.

Elderly Petrol Engine Syndrome is, of course, something you pick up in youth, through repeated heartbreaking betrayals at the hands of temperamental elderly petrol engines in sailing boats. My own case is pretty severe, having been triggered by a Stuart which seized solid in the rocky mouth of Goleen Harbour, County Cork, back in 1978. I might have got over it, but the paranoia was confirmed by another Stuart (admittedly badly installed) which first set fire to the boat's floorboards off Portland Bill, and then jammed itself in Full Ahead as it entered Newhaven Marina. You would not believe how far across a marina pontoon you can get in an Itchen Ferry before someone hits the off-button. Nor how far back you subsequently bounce.

Meanwhile, I had an invigorating trip to St Kilda in the immortal oyster-smack *Kathleen*, during which the lightly marinised London taxi diesel engine, which lurked under the cockpit sole, managed first to get stuck in reverse and then to fail completely and finally in the middle of the Sound of Harris at 0100 on a moonless morning.

Engines, therefore, have always meant trouble. My husband, who has a more upbeat attitude and fewer mental scars, gets slightly irritated by the way I assume the worst and rush for the nearest halyard or boathook whenever our poor innocent Yanmar merely coughs. It is, in fact, a fine engine, but still my old instinct is there, causing me to flinch, and mistrust, and hate it, and refuse to learn anything about its dark working.

Or at least, the instinct *was* there, until at last I went into engine therapy. I had tried the treatment before, sending myself on a diesel maintenance course, but unfortunately the trauma of confronting pistons close up was such that I fell fast asleep and heard almost nothing of the lecture. With the launching of the RYA's engine courses I was inveigled into trying again. And it was a revelation.

By great good luck, there were only three of us on it. By even better luck, it was taught by a cheerful soul called Peter Smith, who had not only spent nine years as a VW-Audi and Ford mechanic, but is a keen sailor who runs the family sea school in Ipswich. So he understood about treachery, and EPES, and exactly how you feel when some great iron swine under your floor pulls a foul, devious stunt on you. But at the same time, he appreciates engines. So he is the perfect mediator in the running battle between sailing yachtsman and yacht engine. The Volvo two-cylinder engine on his workbench had, in fact, been worn out and rebuilt twice, personally, by Peter.

He made us confront its marvels, saying, 'Suck, push bang! Blow!', admiring the elegantly turned swirl-chambers on the pistons, and standing around like drama students, one of us being the fuel tank, another the bulkhead holding the fuel pre-filter. We played with the thermostat and fiddled with the fuel-lift pump. 'Look, there's no sacred mystery,' said Peter. 'Give it fuel, give it air, it works.'

He pleaded the engine's case with us, most eloquently. The poor thing was never a traitor at all; it only asked a fair chance. Hypnotised by Peter's eloquence, I became quite upset at the thought of what an engine suffers; all its beautiful, hidden bits and gizmos being expected to struggle on faithfully with dirty fuel, a dinghy sitting on the air intake and a jellyfish wedged up the back end.

I swore I would never leave harbour again with a perished impeller, and would respect my injectors as trusted friends and colleagues.

The emotional block of EPES is shifted. I appreciate my engine now, can't wait to get back to it and paint its bleed-points with love. I can't actually remember now very much else that I am actually meant to do; but I suppose breaking the psychological barrier is the first step.

Rally Ho!

My New Year resolution (apart from varnishing) is to have more rallies. Be sociable. Raft up to other people, if possible in a giant drunken sunflower formation. Put pelican-hooks in the guardwires so that you can fling them aside hospitably for visitors to step aboard. Create a permanent stowage for at least three wine-boxes, rafted up with shock-cord. Learn to play the concertina. Get a bigger frying pan for jolly communal breakfasts, luring fellow sailors across the chilly morning anchorage with the matchless smell of bacon.

Do I see green gills there, hear indrawn gasps? What do you mean, you go sailing to get away from other people? Are you telling me that if you wanted to go to a drinks party you would stay at home? What was that? You reckon that once you've got a ship, an isle and a sickle moon, the last thing you need is three boat loads of hearty people playing accordions and yarning till dawn with their bums planted firmly on what should be your bunk? Well, yes. I do see your point. Even sympathise, a bit.

For cruising yachtsmen divide into the gregarious and the antiso- cial. Some join yacht clubs for the showers and the slipway, and others join for the laying-up dinner. Some raft up, others anchor off. Far away, with 100m of chain.

Partly, of course, it depends where you cruise. Along the crowded South Coast solitude is precious, and you may well cast a furious jaundiced eye at every swine who comes into Newtown Creek after you. In lonelier waters, another yacht is sheer comfort. When we fled from a nasty gale in Tobermory Harbour once to hide in Loch Drom'na Buidhe, it was in company with a fellow member of the RCC we had only just met.

We were feeling exceedingly sorry for ourselves, up on that coast with horrible weather, and might well have begun to snivel. But Bill and his son swept in alongside us, concluded a fancy anchoring manoeuvre to keep us safely rafted, and spent a couple of hours telling us with roars of laughter about numerous infinitely worse gales through which they had sat, frequently on two anchors. Somehow, we felt the better for it.

And in Dingle once, after spending three miserable nights trembling for our lives in Smerwick Bay, we struck up what was practically a holiday romance with what would (I suspect) have seemed, nearer home, like a really boring boat full of really boring people. It was hard to tear ourselves away.

Then when I wrote about our trip round Britain in 1987, the people we found really hard to forgive were the ones whose letters began: 'We saw you in Loch Horrible in the fog, from our villa, but we thought we would respect your privacy. . .' Ha! Rather have a hot bath than privacy, any day, up Loch Grim.

I was on a boat once in Fécamp, when our burgee was recognised and we were boarded by three masterful men from the same club and a lank-haired girl who had been suborned into cooking for them. At one stage, she and I went into the cockpit to finish drying the dishes, leaving my men and hers below. 'Oohhhhh,' she murmured, polishing a mug, 'you don't know what this means to me. We couldn't talk about clothes, or something, could we? I mean, not sailing clothes?'

Clubbable clubs are an insurance against getting too close to one's shipmates without relief. Lilliput, at Poole, developed its enormous burgee mainly as a device whereby Lilliputians might recognise one another across alien marinas or open anchorages. The Royal Cruising Club burgee generally produces excellent company, even if there is a grave risk that they will have sailed further than you. 'Been far? We've come all the way from Brighton! Oh, I see. How long does it take to get from Lofoten to Gibraltar, exactly?'

But club rallies can turn sour on you. Some friends, in a very pukka old boat, went to a rally once held by the Provisional Wing of

PEYTON

the Old Gaffers' Association and fell among purists. She was doing her washing-up in the cockpit in a red plastic bowl, and the chatelaine of the boat next door leaned across and said in hushed tones, 'Oh dear, you'd better borrow our canvas one in the morning. We've got a spare.'

But the real import of my resolution is that I want to sail in places where human company is rare enough always to be welcome. Or, at least, to have some good horror stories to tell. One season ended with a remarkable rally up the Butley River involving two sailing cruisers, a motorboat, a Drascombe lugger, a Mirror, numerous small children and a labrador which had hurt its foot and wore a plastic bag on its paw. It had to be rowed ashore for every wee across acres of slimy mud without getting the foot wet. In the morning, in the rain, there was only one frying-pan between all of us and the motorboat had vanished at dawn in a cloud of marital vituperation. Ah, memories, memories. Roll on summer.

We are Spacemen

I have seen the film *Apollo 13*, the story of the aborted 1970 attempt to land on the Moon, three times. While the age of my son has a lot to do with this, I do not repine: it still pins me to my seat every time. Partly, I suppose, this is because during the years of the early moonshots I was far too left-wing, feminist, etc to take any interest in the boys' toys at NASA, so I missed the adventure first time round. But while I was watching Tom Hanks and the lads being thrown all over the module as they tried to use their unreliable thrusters to get back on to the right track for Port Earth, I suddenly realised that there was another reason. Not many critics have noticed this, but *Apollo 13* is all about sailing.

This first became apparent when my husband and then 12-year-old son tried to explain to me about all the business with the docking and the lunar module. 'The spaceship has to dock in space, right, and collect the lunar landing module,' they began. Seeing my blank face, they revised it. 'Look, someone's left them a dinghy on a mooring in space, and they have to pick up the mooring and collect the dinghy so that they can – er, row ashore on the Moon. The spaceship – yacht, if you like – can't land on the Moon, so they need the module as a dinghy. Then when the main yacht fails, they finally have to use it as a lifeboat to get back to Earth!'

Fair enough. But, of course, it goes further. Everything about the Apollo 13 mission echoes the experience of sailing. There they are, in harbour at NASA, surrounded by all the latest wonderful high-tech equipment, by advisers and Mission Control Harbourmasters and great shedsful of space chandlery. They prepare everything, draw up a passage plan, get their foul-weather spacesuits on and set off on the preordained tide, aiming to anchor off the Moon and land. As if it were, say, Sark. Then they plan to dance around a bit in the sand before bringing home some rock for the kiddies.

But when it is far too late to turn back, the equipment starts to go wrong. It was a coil which overheated in some obscure corner of *Apollo*; just as a spreader might snap, or a chainplate pull out, or a seacock fracture. From that moment on, the only things which can save the crew are cool heads, determination, inventiveness and judgement. See them struggling against panic, cobbling up air filters out of socks and plastic bags and grey tape. Who has not done much the same, in a heaving swell, against the clock? See them making, with Mission Control, the difficult decision not to turn right round, but to use the fair tide of the Moon's gravitational pull to 'slingshot' back towards Earth; for all the world like any of us making a seamanlike decision to stand offshore rather than risk a dangerous run for a lee shore.

See them hauling at the helm, their unreliable thrust engines, with all the navigational equipment down and their only guide the need to keep the mark – the Earth – in the middle of the window as they manoeuvre. Finally, see them with their jury rig roaring and juddering through re-entry, worrying about the heat-shield. The astronauts' set, white faces at this point will be only too familiar to anybody who has ever glanced around at the rest of a yacht crew while crossing Salcombe Bar in a southerly.

You see? They were just yachting in space. Or, to put it another way, every time one of us sets out to sea we partake in our modest way of all the great adventures since the beginning of time: exploration and experiment, lonely risks taken in desert, jungle, ocean and glacier. We have to prepare carefully but accept that things might let us down; we have to know enough to reinvent the whole plan in a hurry, in the dark, in order to get back safely at all.

The only thing we lack is Mission Control; and even that is mimicked to a point by GPS – advice from space to Earth, instead of the other way round – and the weather forecast. Our routine mission might end in no greater step for mankind than a trip up the Cherbourg pontoons for a *fruits-de-mer* and a bilgeful of plonk. But it might, without warning, turn into a crisis of life and death.

Staggering from the cinema seat, undoing my imaginary harness, I reflected that this is probably why a lot of us do it. We are more than just Walter Mittys, because however sensible and cautious we are, the sea is real and therefore the adventure is real too. Sailing is one of the few ways in which an ordinary, deskbound and not particularly athletic Westerner can partake of the ancient, honourable, awesome world of self-reliant adventure. And even take the children along, too.

In a world of vicarious thrills and Virtual Reality this is no small thing. It is something which those who sneer at pampered yachties and their tinkling boats never quite understand. Inside the harbour we may be ludicrous hobbyists, but 10 miles out to sea we have a share in the oldest terrors and triumphs of all. We are spacemen.

The Tank of Virtue

April: things will have changed by now; the daffs could be up and the wind down. We may even have finished the varnishing and got the mattresses and cushions and books and booze aboard to bring the boat back to life. But as I write this, the days are dank and the Rummer is a shambles. Once a week, we go to the boatyard where blue-nosed lads huddle round a black woodstove the size of a Mini. We climb the ladder and look down through the hatch to see how the work on galley and fo'c'sle and engine is getting on, and I – pathetic female creature, unable to look beyond the surface of things – gulp.

For the floor yawns open to the empty engine compartment, there are cables and lights and vacuum-cleaners littered around, unfinished racks and fiddles lying dismally on the chart table, shavings on the floor, daylight shining in through unsettling holes and twists of plastic pipe poking up through others. She is not the dignified and seaman-like boat we fell in love with in a Falmouth Harbour heatwave; she feels small and grubby and chaotic.

Which, of course, is entirely as it should be. It was the same when *Grace O'Malley* was being built in the same yard; all boats look less than half-finished until the magic day when they are, quite suddenly, ready. I gather that in swanky South Coast yards they sweep up and put back the floorboards before the owner's visits, and therefore have to discourage random visiting; here the opposite is true. We turn up any time; they don't mind, and we have to face the creative jumble. Paul rather enjoys this, being quite a handy workman himself, but I – although I know perfectly well really what goes on under boats' floorboards – am DIY illiterate and therefore rattled. It is like going to see a loved one in hospital: you know that the tubes up his nose, the drip, the colostomy bag and the shaven head are all signs of expert care. But all the same . . .

Moreover, in this particular case, the Rummer's ordeal has been prolonged by an expensive and awkward bit of elective surgery. When we bought her, she had a chemical lavatory; beautifully clean and thoughtfully installed, but somehow so innately depressing that one dark night up the Fal we shook hands, solemnly, on an agreement to get rid of our green plastic shipmate as soon as possible. I think it was the little squeegee concertina flushing device that finished me off. That, and a grave doubt as to how long its bijou tank could last with four people on long passages. We wanted a pumping sea-toilet, and the reassuring suck and swish of inner cleanliness.

But the chemical khazi set us thinking. The last owner had put it in on principle: he lives in West Cornwall. The Cornish water is clear and sparkling, and invites not only the cruising sailor but the swimmer, the surfer, the boardsailor, snorkeller and diver. None of us is pleased with the government and water authority record on polluting UK beaches with sewage: so what makes us think we can pump our sea-toilets at anchor? Especially now that there are so many of us?

It was different in the 1940s, when there might be only two or three yachts up the Helford or in a quiet cove, discreetly manipulating their Baby Blakes. Today we are legion. It is the difference between one shy mouse leaving droppings in your larder, and an invasion of enormous incontinent rats. It won't do. Not any longer. Frankly, if British waters were not so murky and so rapidly tidal, there would have been an outcry against yachtsmen long ago. In the next few years, I suspect there will be.

So we resolved to pre-empt criticism, scale the moral high ground and have a holding-tank: the kind where you hoard the stuff in harbour, and only pump it out five miles offshore where it can more readily disperse. Apart from anything else, it would be a powerful incentive to go to sea. We were not, however, terribly keen on a flexible tank. Not since we met the Mediterranean flotilla engineer who told us of the crew who got their valves muddled and for a

whole week thought they were pumping it clear while really they were just pressurising it up. In the end it was 'Thar she blows!' as the whole thing erupted; its aged, atomised contents coated the boat and crew. Nervously, we opted for stainless steel, shaped to fit the elegant but not roomy bow curves of this 1960s boat.

So – as I write – the fo'c'sle is chaos. There is a seawater inlet pipe and a toilet outflow pipe; this forks to provide either a clear pump-out or a route to the holding tank. From the tank there is another outflow doubling back towards the exit seacock; and then there is the breather. At each junction there are valves. We are assured by the lads that it will all be beautifully tidied away in a week or two, but right now the whole thing looks like an imaginative diagram of the lower intestine drawn by Heath Robinson on LSD.

A sinister white box dominates the fo'c'sle. We know that visitors will ask 'What's in there?' We know that we should be proud to answer frankly, but have not thought of a way to put it. Maybe we will just reply, 'Our conscience'.

Crude Crew • 1

It was Des Sleightholme who first pointed out that ashore it is not considered polite to set weekend guests a strict luggage limit and then greet them on arrival with a jovial instruction to bed down in the cupboard under the stairs, or squeeze behind the hot water tank in the attic for the night on an inch of foam rubber mat. Whereas on a boat we say, 'You'll be snug enough in the quarterberth, Brenda, and there's a bin bag to put over your feet if it rains. Jack, you're in the pipe cot over me, just don't bring your knees up sharply or you'll have the lamp-glass on the floor.'

If they have been misled by the word 'yacht' to expect something smoother, this may rattle them as it rattled Carruthers in *The Riddle of the Sands*, when he completed his 'sordid midnight scramble over damp meat and littered packing-cases' and found himself in the head-bumping, dripping, rabbit-hutch cabin of Davies's boat.

The unprepared lay visitor is thrown even further off course over dinner by sinister instructions like 'Jack, could you just get the fruit salad out? It's in a plastic box under the floorboards in the fo'c'sle. That's it, just by where your feet go when you sit on the Lavac.' Or 'Just pass me an onion, could you, Belinda, from under Paul's wellies.'

At sea, things do not get much better, as we absently explain that

the log is jammed and cannot be cleared unless the flexible water tank is half empty, which should be around Wednesday; but that it hardly matters because 'we generally do 4 knots, give or take, and you always know when you surge over 5 knots because seawater spouts up through the sink plug'. And we shall draw a veil over the effect of a first encounter with a really well-seasoned Baby Blake in a lively head sea. One renowned woman TV presenter once went sailing with her editor and – according to him – took one look at the facilities and 'never Went, for two whole days'.

Our old Contessa had a transparent loop of piping behind the heads through which pink paper could be seen flying past at eye level as one pumped. It frightened off several shipmates before we finally obscured it with black tape.

This embarking of strangers is always a nervous business: even if they are only strangers to the boat, being well-loved friends ashore. They might say that they want to come sailing, but be so revolted by the reality of it that they go right off you, and tell the whole office the intimate horrors of your fo'c'sle. One colleague came out with us for a weekend and got quite savage. 'I hate this,' he said bitterly. 'Nothing with a proper name. The floor is the sole and the roof is the deckhead and I'm not allowed to say front and back. I'm now frightened to ask for a teaspoon in case it's called something different at sea.'

Think how miserable he would have been on an OGA rally, with people bellowing at him to reeve the jib-tops'l tackline back under the gammon and round the bitts. I once had a boyfriend who would never say 'Put the cabin light out please,' but barked, 'Hoy, dowse that glim!' We did not last long.

For I know the process from both ends: having no family sailing background, I spent my youth bamboozling my way on to a series of yachts with no prior experience. Getting used to sleeping on shelves was no problem, and I actually enjoyed the language. But I can tell you that the really unnerving bit is the way that skippers constantly assess you. This is not part of normal social currency either: when you go to someone's house they do not narrow their eyes and visibly calculate the odds on your falling downstairs and being unable to work the shower.

It was a relief when they were frank. 'Well, Libby,' enquired one skipper, 'is it worth showing you how to do things properly, or not? If you're never coming again, I shan't waste effort on you.' On my humbly saying I would come again, I was handed down his personal, lapidary shipboard rules. These burned themselves into my mind so deeply that to this day, if I see anyone putting a jamming- hitch on a halyard cleat, I faint with horror.

More difficult are the skippers who try stealthily to find out whether you are going to be any use. A favourite ploy is to give you the helm immediately, mutter 'follow the red buoys out,' and then crouch in the cabin peering nervously through the portholes to see whether you push the stick the right way. They also long to find out whether you are going to be a liability. As another frank host said on a windy night: 'Look, if you find you can't cope, just for God's sake find your own bucket, wrap up warm and keep out of the way.' Ashore, he was the soul of *politesse* and chivalry.

But comfortingly, in the end the popular crew is the one who is the best company during the long boring bits. For this you forgive boots in the companionway, wasted fresh water and erratic steering. We once had a friend so well-meaningly insistent on standing his watch, and so dangerously inefficient when he did, that on a wild night in the Thames Estuary we found him steering a reciprocal course due to a misunderstanding of the grid compass. Rather than offend him, Paul felled this particular rogue elephant with the equivalent of a tranquilliser dart: spiking his cocoa with so much whisky that he crashed out until morning. He came again, though. We liked him.

Wind-up

My favourite Christmas present a few years back was a clockwork radio. I have wanted one ever since I met its inventor, Trevor Baylis, on the *Midweek* programme on Radio 4.

Now, it must be admitted that this programme airs a lot of inventive ideas, and some of them are pretty flaky. This was different. Think about it: radio broadcasting is a vital way for the world to keep itself informed, entertained – and democratic. BBC World Service is a major force for good. Yet in remote regions with no mains power, precisely where news is most important, batteries are like gold-dust and radios lie silent for months while the next consignment of Duracells is exchanged for wildebeest steaks or camel milk 100 miles away.

Mr Baylis thought, 'Well – transistors don't use all that much power, and we all waste a lot of energy just waving our arms around, so why not give these people wind-up radios?'

There were technical reasons why not: that the mechanism of spring and cogs translating into instant electricity would interfere with reception; that you need a constant steady supply of power, because it wouldn't work if it ran down slower and slower like a clockwork toy; and, not least, that manufacturers doubled up and shrieked with laughter at the very idea.

Mr Baylis persisted, solved the technical problems, found a manufacturer, and the rest is history. Baygen radios are being proudly carted around all over the third world, their neat little folding handles at one end.

I do not live in the bush, but find mine deeply satisfying for more Western reasons. Like chopping logs or trimming sails, it meets an atavistic urge to *earn* a result, physically, rather than just sucking up fossil fuels and pushing buttons. It restores the listener's dignity.

Instead of being a passive recipient of broadcasting, you become a decision-maker. A brisk bout of wristwork supplies, say, the 0700 news and *The Archers*, or half *The World at One*. Then it stops and you decide whether the rest of the show is worth the effort of winding up for. No longer do you deplete the world's resources listening to things which only annoy you.

The yachting implications first sank in when Mike Richey, low-tech sailor extraordinaire, laid eyes on the machine. A man who regularly takes 50 days to cross the Atlantic in an engineless boat

was instantly beguiled by the idea of unrationed shortwave. As his eyes lit up, it struck me like a thunderbolt that here was the answer to several problems: the lack of exercise on long passages, the difficulty of finding anything for bored crew to do once the sails are set, and the greed for power of yacht electrics. Clockwork is the answer!

So I rang Trevor Baylis, who instantly told me about his latest radio. Its power supply is not a spring, but hauling a bucket of water up a tall tree in the morning and letting it slowly descend. 'Masts!' he cried. 'Boats have masts! Pull up a canvas bag full of water . . .'

I pointed out that the slow descent of a big wet bag from a tall mast in a heavy swell could have drawbacks, and he reluctantly concurred. However, we agreed that some yachtie appliances would be ideal for clockwork power: for isolated soundings an echo sounder only needs to deliver a short sharp burst of power: a quick wind-up as you approached the mud on each tack would do the trick.

VHF might be slightly more trouble, as transmitting uses far more power than receiving; but you could develop a hybrid, which used spring-power for the reception, amplification and display, but a battery for transmission. GPS could be contrived, he reckons, and even a clockwork EPIRB is not out of the question: 'It could generate a special code so that people knew it was a mechanical device – clear the way, here's an emergency.' We started discussing logs, but then realised that a Walker trailing log already is, effectively, clockwork.

Navigation lights, of course, are another matter. I had assumed that the power drain would be too great, but Mr Baylis was optimistic. He already has a torch giving 1W for 15 minutes on a brief winding, and was quite happy to think bigger.

'After all,' he said, 'There's no need for a built-in appliance on a yacht to be portable, is there? You could have a *very, very powerful spring*, in its own metal case, with a sophisticated gearbox. That could be a terrific power resource. Imagine it, down in the bilges amongst the ballast, with some big blokes up top putting in some yo-ho-ho on the windlass before dusk . . .'

We dreamed on. Solar panels, we agreed, were OK for topping up batteries, but 'Not much use in Lapland in winter, are they? I'm trying to show that you really can get through life without batteries. All I need is for someone to enlighten me on the special needs of maritime users, and there we go . . .'

And off he went, to finesse some secret new project. I carried on dreaming of a day when teenagers, beefy brothers-in-law and bored fitness freaks will provide all the power a yacht could desire, winding and grinding the lights, the instruments, the self-steering, the fridge, the microwave . . .

I have just noticed which issue this is going to be published in April. Bother. You think it's a joke, don't you? A wind-up? Hah! Wait and see. We will show you one day, Mr Baylis and I.

Keel Pride

A few years ago the fabulous narcotic high brought on by the resinous smells and neon colours of Earls Court was rather rudely dispelled. Just as each new wave of Boat Show optimism and techno-lust was having its giddy way with us, up came another story from the Southern Ocean, where the boats in the Vendée Globe were circling Antarctica and occasionally revolving on their own axis. Earls Court was not entirely fazed by this, it was good to see the quick-thinking EPIRB salesmen popping up on the News to show their modern Aladdin's lamps which, when rubbed, conjure up not genies but big reassuring Aussie frigates.

But by and large, there was an unwelcome sobering effect in watching the first three crises. The heroism of Pete Goss's rescue of Raphael Dinelli was fine: yacht gets in trouble, other rescues it, fifteen-all, and the honour of the sport upheld. However, discomfort began to mount with the capsize and rescue of both Thierry Dubois and the astonishing Tony Bullimore. Of course it was exhilarating when our Tony tapped his message to the saviours hammering on the hull: that was the good bit. But meanwhile there had been – not to put too fine a point on it altogether – too many aerial pictures of yachts floating peacefully on the briny *the wrong way up*.

Dubois's boat was the worst example, especially for those like myself who are earnestly trying to cast off years of baggywrinkled Luddism and learn to appreciate radical modern yacht design. When you have been schlepping around the Boat Show, weaning yourself off bowsprits and straight stems by admiring the sculptural beauty of wide skimming boats with short, dashing keels, the last thing you need is endless TV pictures of an equally graceful boat upside-down, with her pretty little spindly keel pointing skyward and a morose-looking Frenchman standing next to it like someone trying to explain an exhibit at the Tate Modern.

I am no naval architect, but the fact that, despite the waves, the damn thing stayed comfortably upside-down was distinctly unnerving. Even when racing dinghies capsize on the Alde and don't pop up, it usually turns out that either the board has fallen out or the mast is buried half a metre deep in the mud. Since this seems unlikely in the Southern Ocean, the lay mind is forced to conclude that there just isn't enough weight down there (I mean, up there) in the keel to convince the boat that she would be more comfortable the right way up. With multihulls, it is at least obvious: you can see straightaway that a capsize will be more or less permanent and you take care accordingly. With a monohull, the natural expectation is that she will somehow want to come upright. When she doesn't, you get unhappy.

At least Tony Bullimore's keel had the grace to fall off, and not poke jauntily in the air; but that caused twinges of alarm in its own right. 'Came off like a matchstick,' he said cheerfully after his rescue. But if there is one thing the cautious cruising mind clings to, it is the idea that, by and large, the keel is not an optional fal-lal which could fall off. Worrying about masts and rudder is quite enough, thank you, without fretting about the bloody keel. Of course since then there have been proper enquiries, made by proper chaps with computers, into why these things keep happening. There were also dour voices saying 'they never did learn the lessons of the Fastnet, did they?' and progressive voices saying nonsense, radical designs can be safe, fine calculations have been made, and racing boats routinely survive far worse conditions than cruisers.

I am unqualified to take sides, and accept that racers will always push the limits. But since cruising design inevitably follows racing innovation (just look around any boat show), all I can offer is the voice of cruising instinct. In that voice, quavering a bit at the image of Dubois communing with his useless underpinning 1,000 miles from anywhere, all I can do is gibber: *Gimme a great big keel! Bigger the better! One that points downwards!*

And, moreover, one which looks right. One which, when you see the boat dried out, is comfortably integral to her shape. In old wooden boats you can watch the whole strength of the structure flowing outward from the keel, growing like a flower from its root. 'Ah yes!' you think, slapping on gallon after gallon of anti-fouling as if you were lathering a hippo, 'It looks right, it is right!' And you can

keep beer cold in the bilges. And it doesn't go bang-slappety-bang on waves. Secretly, I like a full old-fashioned keel with just one grudging cut-out for the propeller. Lesser keels will do, providing they have the appearance of being at the heart of the designer's thinking, rather than petulantly slapped on afterwards. However, this point of view is not chic; not in the presence of those who would rather mess about with wings and bulbs than the majestic underwater barn doors of yesteryear. Big keels do not have a cool image. Maybe we need a campaign of macho bragging. 'Mark Fishwick – what a hunk! It takes a real man to handle a keel like that!' And: 'Phwooarr – you won't catch Tom Cunliffe with some Barbie-doll fin – he can take all the lead you can bolt on!' Big keels must stand up and be counted. Or rather, stay down, where you can't see them.

What Saves You

Oh hell, they are at it again. Not the EC this time, but the UN, of all normally reasonable bodies. It seems, from a newspaper I found stuck to the varnish can, that certain European countries wish us to take tests and brandish certificates before we presume to sail their coasts and waterways.

The countries most vocal on the subject do not immediately strike

me as shining examples of yacht seamanship, but let that pass: it is
not for me to point the finger at Russians weaving around the
Channel in homemade galleons with dodgy compasses, at
Frenchmen whose anchoring technique is to hurl a CQR over the
toerail at 6 knots and see what happens, or at Germans who hog the
centre of a 40ft outside marina berth in a boat the size of a large egg
cup and then send big blonde women up to shriek at anybody trying
to creep alongside in the grim Ramsgate dawn.

But they may win. It takes very little to persuade modern govern-
ments to make tests compulsory for every human activity. It could be
that, by the time this is published, we shall all be glumly preparing
to take driving tests before we attempt the perilous waters of the
IJsselmeer or the treacherous entrance to Cherbourg (remember,
class: the solid grey bit is the breakwater, and the bit you can see
through is the entrance).

Even worse, maybe we shall have to show licences to sail our
own waters. The suggestion is that it should be modelled on the car
driving test: even now, a labyrinthine building full of doomed computers could be going up in Swansea and civil servants combing the
land for a sufficient number of grey, depressed, snappish, dyspeptic
retired policemen to serve as examiners.

Now me, I am a confirmed poltroon: the kind of person who
thinks it folly to go out in anything over
Force 4, alters course three miles away
from teeny trawlers, and prefers to
approach all berths at half a knot while
festooned from bow to quarter with a
world-beating collection of exotic
fenders. I should be dead keen on
anything that makes sailing safer. But
somehow the idea of a yacht driving
test has always left me cold. I cannot begin to see what good it
would do.

The parallel with the driving
test just does not work: actual
control of the car is a
fairly small part of that
test, and the bit that
makes drivers safer is
reading the road,
responding sensibly

PRYTON

52

to other traffic, and knowing the rigid, but well-signposted and unvarying, disciplines of junctions and roundabouts. How are you going to test the myriad disciplines that a yacht skipper needs, among unsignposted sandbanks and infinitely variable rocks and currents?

After all, nobody is suggesting that these tests would be anywhere near as rigorous or time-consuming as the full RYA Yachtmaster, which is the closest we have to a good test; and even qualified Yachtmasters (saving their reverence) have been known to get into pretty silly kinds of trouble. A more basic, universal test would be ludicrously useless; worse, because it would give unwarranted confidence to people who passed it. The best safety device of all is a wholesome fear of the sea.

You can prove, in an artificial test setting, that somebody can do a three-point turn out of a marina berth, or come alongside at a wharf or in a lock – but you can't create a brisk wind up the tail, or a spring tide, or reconstruct the emotional state of somebody who has been up all night in a rolling sea trying to fix a starter motor with a torch held between his teeth.

Anyway, the kind of manoeuvring that can easily be tested is not the skill which most bad yachtsmen lack. Some of the biggest idiots offshore are very good indeed at picking up moorings. I would concede that drivers of high-speed powerboats (and wetbikes, yah!) should take some kind of handling test, and carry licences which could be removed if they play the goat once too often; but a cruising boat wallowing along at low speeds under sail or feeble motor is not much threat to anyone, and the skills of its skipper are untestable.

If I count up the things which have saved us from peril on the sea they are, in order of appearance:

1. Paul's ability to bleed a diesel at immense speed, on pure adrenaline, in a narrow sound.
2. A bout of cowardice resulting in an extra evening in the pub.
3. The power of prayer resulting in the merciful lifting of an unforecast veil of fog off Inishbofin.
4. A very tenacious anchor and more cowardice.
5. A muttered decade of the rosary, resulting in the wind holding out for just long enough to ghost in to Loch Aline with a ruptured fuel pipe.

None of these things would be easy for an examiner to pin down. But it is notable that not once were our lives saved by a fancy display of prop-walking, a talent for rattling off the meanings of flags, or an ability to see the point of those tidal curves that look like bits of Pamela Anderson.

Grande Luxe

I'll say one thing about Saddam Hussein; he had discreet boat-builders. Normally, in my experience, any yard with a commission to build an interesting yacht finds it impossible to resist showing it off to the curious. Many's the ladder I have crept up, egged on by a beaming chippie, to ooh and aah at some dreamboat's joinery. But Saddam stationed army chaps with bulging armpits and shades around a certain Finnish yard, so it took a great many years for details of the 1982 completion of his yacht *al-Mansur* to be leaked to a curious world.

Worth the wait, though: 106m, 12,000hp, satellite gizmos, anti-bugging devices, a 200-place banqueting hall and solid gold taps in the stateroom. The delivery skipper, Captain Peter Schauman, said lightly to a newspaper, 'Since then I've never been impressed at a Boat Show'. But then, to be fair, he only knew the ship when she was brand new and presumably everything was working properly. Gold is a soft metal: bet you anything that solid gold taps drip like hell, causing the electric pump motor to whir on in the middle of the night and enrage the dozing dictator as he tries to get some kip after a long day's wielding of absolute power.

There is something strangely fascinating about vast luxury afloat. The audiences who queued down every High Street for the movie *Titanic* did not really want to see a film about the need for better watertight bulkheads and lifeboat capacity in 1915. Still less were they anxious for a soupy teenage love affair drawn out to 140 minutes before the merciful intervention of Brother Iceberg.

What they came for was to see a creation of fantastic opulence and luxury and taste and comfort going glug-glug-glug to the bottom of the ocean. Like all those shots in old epic movies of palaces crumbling in earthquakes, it satisfied some deep, obscure need. From this point of view the most satisfying thing that could happen to Saddam's gold taps would be for them to end up on the sea-bed of the Shatt-al-Arab, to be found by divers 50 years later with barnacles up their spout.

Yachtsmen, of course, have an ambivalent attitude to both things:

the luxury and the sinking. We like to disparage showy luxury
aboard boats (note my cheap crack above about the gold taps). As
for the sinking, we would rather not think about that at all. People
who never set foot in a boat may get their kicks from watching great
ships upending and sliding under, but we of the yacht club outing
frankly preferred to sink our noses into the remainder of the pop-
corn and not look.

But as we trudged thoughtfully out of the cinemas after *Titanic*
into the viciously cold winter gales, some of us had secretly to admit
that the very reason we are uneasy about sumptuous vessels is
because of the business about sinking, and cold green water rushing
in. When you are defying an alien element, anything but the smallest
home comfort feels like tempting fate. Some of us still even have the
greatest difficulty in accepting the modern trend for velvety Dralon-
type bunk covers on small boats. The old vinyl had something
humble and unassuming about it, fit to placate the angry gods of the
storm. Dralon says 'I am as safe as if I were ashore'. Plastic says 'Er,
look, I do realise that my bunk might get wet. I admit that there's
water out there, and that it makes no promises'.

The same goes for the galley – all the biscuits tucked into
Tupperware, even for the shortest trip across the bay, and the snap
tops fitted properly on the teabag caddy – and for electrics. I sailed
on a boat once which had a pressurised electric water system and –
get this – absolutely no alternative way of extracting water from the
main tank without taking up the entire floor and sucking it out

through a straw. And it feels plain arrogant to have a yacht under 15m which would be seriously disabled or lost if its batteries should go funny. Bigger than that I suppose you can have a standby generator. Or perhaps two. In waterproof boxes.

Maybe I am superstitious, but at sea soft luxury feels dangerous, as if the attention of the designer and crew has been unforgivably distracted from the central business of arriving at the destination, floating. It does not have to be uncomfortable or ugly below, but a certain decent sparseness feels safer. Even on ferries and cruise ships I do not want a huge round bed with fun-fur trimmings. I want a narrow, dry bunk with a rail to stop me falling out; a rail whose presence also silently acknowledges that stabilisers are not infallible and that the sea is perfectly within its rights to roll us around.

A modest interior feels – well, decent. And it has practical advantages. I met a Welsh chap once whose elderly gaffer sank majestically on its mooring. He generally took his few instruments home in his bag after a cruise, so only the VHF suffered. Otherwise her refloating with a repaired seacock was 'No problem really – we dried out the bunks, chucked some fresh water around down below and let the wind through her for a week. Sweet as a nut.'

Think how nasty your round leopardskin bed and padded leatherette headlining would have smelt, after a week at the bottom of Milford Haven . . .

Pessimists and Pilots

Is it the duty of a pilot book to encourage, or to deter? Or should it remain blandly neutral and list the harbour lights? If you are approaching Madman's Bay, do you want an eager companion by your side, enthusing about the rare rock formations and excellent pub, or a pessimist fretting about kelp and potential swell in strong SSE winds? When you are listening to the wind and rain across the cabin top the night before and planning your next dash across open water, is it more important that your invisible guide takes a sanguine view of yachting, or that he (it always is a he, isn't it?) remembers to point out every single disadvantage of your destination?

These are not idle questions. There are people even now sitting down to write pilot books, and they have to make their minds up what tone to take and how much common sense to expect of the reader. The pilot must decide whether to encourage the punter, and

risk being blamed if
he doesn't enjoy
Deadhaddock Creek
after all; or to take
such an artfully
miserable approach
to every haven that
the navigator is
surprised even to
survive it.

The author's deci-
sion, believe me,
will affect the
amateur navigator a
good deal. It is
pointless pretending
that we only look to
pilot books for the
chartlets and the tidal streams: most of us are more insecure than
that, and want a guiding word as well. So there are volumes on the
chandlers' shelves which can radically affect a cruise, and make
much of the difference between a pleasant adventure and a fortnight
of buttock-clenching tension.

Of the classics, the tone of Adlard Coles is measured but adventur-
ous, and respectful of the reader; it would be hard to take exception
to it. Mark Fishwick strikes the same kind of balance, bolstered by
the comforting inside knowledge that frankly, if you can get
Temptress's vast depth of keel into a harbour, you can get anything
in short of *Ark Royal*. But if these occupy the middle ground of optimism, there are also extremes.

Take the Irish Cruising Club's famous *Sailing Directions* to the
South and West Coasts of their island. These are wild coasts, to be
approached with seriousness and caution, and the book does not
underplay this in any way. Yet from the first page it breathes optimism: St Columba, 563 AD, is the first authority quoted, saying '*What
joy to sail the crested sea and watch the waves beat white upon the
Irish shore*'. Every anchorage, even the most dubious, is seen to have
compensations: ' . . . *a good harbour but subject to roll in southerly
winds. Its north-west arm is wooded and very attractive*'. Or again '*No
marks at the entrance, but a splendid shelter. Exit impossible in bad
weather*'. Whole tracts of coast are excused their deficiencies of
shopping and lighthouses with comfortable assurances that fog is

rare and the inhabitants friendly. The phrase 'endless scope for exploration' is brought into play where a glummer book would talk only of poor VHF coverage. As I say, this is no coast for nervous beginners, and the book does not make it seem so; but nonetheless, optimism and adventure breathe off every page.

But then take the not dissimilar coast of the Western Isles of Scotland, and observe the dour Caledonian approach, '*This book*', says the author, the admirably conscientious but far from joyful Martin Lawrence, '*is not trying to "sell" the West Coast.*'

Indeed it is not. Although he mentions splendid scenery at intervals, there is always head-shaking about squalls off the mountains; if an anchorage is good you are warned that it will be crowded, and if it is lonely then the odds are that there is swell, or fishing nets, or a drying reef. The Lynn of Lorn has '*tides running strongly and a need for careful pilotage*', but if this sends you to the Lynn of Morvern instead, you find that it has '*neither the pilotage problems nor the interest of the Lynn of Lorn*'. Most anchorages are far from shops and services, but when you get to Fort William it '*has nothing to offer the yachtsman except the convenience of shops and some services*'. Tobermory is damned for soft mud and the fact that fishing boats sometimes pinch the visitors' moorings; Mr Lawrence has no qualms about dismissing a whole loch as '*not particularly interesting*'. I repeat, the book is useful and the only full pilot to this patch of water, for which we all owe it some gratitude. But it does cast a certain pall of gloom.

Between the impish enthusiasm of the Irish pilot and the glumness of the Scots, there are infinite gradations of optimism and *brio*. The current armchair reading in this house is Armitage's and Brackenbury's *Norwegian Cruising Guide*, which, despite its detailed guidance on what kind of semi-automatic rifle to carry in case of massed polar bear attack, takes the kind of cheery approach which says, '*Delightful yacht anchorage . . . enclosing, sheltering spit . . . east winds may fill it with drift ice . . . colony of little auks believed to number 250,000*'. Or '*Possible laundry here. Watch overhead cable heights. Disco near visitors' berths*'. You feel that even as you tried to shoot icebergs with your semi-automatic rifle to the wild disco beat of an Arctic rave, the authors would be with you in spirit, saying 'Isn't this an adventure?' rather than 'Told you so!' It makes a difference; it really does.

Marina Shock

The anchor lives cat-headed on the bow, and to our immense surprise it stayed there, all the way from Gigha to Kinsale. Never in the history of a 10 days' cruise has our fo'c'sle so bewilderingly failed to reek of rotting seaweed and dubious mud brought up by the chain. Never has the windlass stood so idle, and never has the sterndeck been so depressingly cluttered with fenders, like a nest of fat white slugs. Normally we can boot them up the forepeak and forget them.

But leaving the Hebrides after a couple of seasons there and one up the west coast of Ireland, we suddenly found ourselves back in marinas and fish-docks and ferryports. We had lain to a pontoon on Kerrera, but otherwise been anchored or moored for nearly three years, even taking on most of our fuel in cans from the dinghy via the mizzen-halyard. Arriving at Bangor Marina, frankly, we felt like peasants, fumbling with ropes and giant slugs and trying to remember where our stern fairleads used to be before we thoughtlessly stowed the inflatable on top of them.

It was a great culture-shock. After so many wild anchorages, coming into a marina is a very different experience. We had forgotten, for example, the irresistible urge to eat out and the deep reluctance to cook. Arriving in an anchorage on a wild damp night, it is a positive pleasure to remember that you have got two pairs of kippers stashed away in a plastic bag under the loose cabin floorboard. Arriving in a huge, smart marina with tidy showered people mincing along the pontoons in designer boatwear, the

PEYTON

kippers start to feel less like a hidden treasure and more like a shameful secret.

Then there is the washing thing. When you are grappling daily with lumps of sea-bed, and rowing damply ashore to the lights of the island pub, washing is what you do merely to prevent yourself smelling. Or, at least, smelling any worse than the anchor chain. Presented with state-of-the-art power showers and walls of mirrors, you go into a frenzy of hygiene. Then you get back to the boat and suddenly notice that your bedding is not of the freshest, and that the clothes you gaily washed in a bucket lack a certain professional finish. Your whole perspective shifts, and looking at the sleek white craft around you, you perceive your beloved boat as a floating slum.

The other curiosity is the way that marinas present themselves. In return for vast sums of money you are solemnly handed a booklet about the harbour and the town, full of esoteric and uplifting information but with absolutely no clue as to where you might find fresh milk and a newspaper on a Sunday night. Years ago, we sailed into the wet-dock at Penzance where a cheerful Harbourmaster's assistant took our lines and yelled, 'You'll find Tesco is just by the gasometer, and there's a launderette up to the right.' That is what I call information. If he had been trained in the civic philosophy which produces marina booklets he would have yelled, 'The town is twinned with Hasbijn, Holland, and St Julien-sans-Culottes in Brittany, and boasts a fine Museum of the Scallop, which was opened in June 1992 by Princess Michael of Kent.'

Anyway, we did not carp, but bounced from one fine marina to the next all the way down to Arklow, where the fish-dock beckoned. Again, we had forgotten about the cosy, niffy business of snuggling up to deserted trawlers, crossing reeking decks and getting hernias trying to haul the great maundering loose-tied lumps near enough to the dock to jump. We had also forgotten, as we progressed along the fishing harbours, about rafting and the eternal horror of the Yacht Just Inside.

This yacht, tied with anally-retentive tightness to the trawler, inevitably declares itself committed to the early tide. 'Fine,' you say. 'We're staying till the later one, but we'll get up and slip the lines, whenever.' The next morning at 0600 an explosive roar shatters your dreams as his engine starts. You spring dutifully from your pit, pull on dew-damp clothes and get to work taking off the springs.

'Oh no,' he says over the roaring. 'We'll be leaving about seven. Just running the engine a bit.'

Then there are the big ferry ports. You spend the night haunted by phantom bursts of enormous wash, the creaking of bow doors, and those booming announcements they like to make in plasticised female voices: 'Bing bong. Ladies and gentlemen, we are now docking in Rosslare. All remaining passengers should make their way to the car decks. Thank you for travelling with Bigshot Scandinavia Ferries. Bing bong! Please ensure that all your personal belongings are taken with you. Bing bong! Will a Mr C Lion please report to the passenger information desk.'

After five or six of these you hurtle on deck in indecent nightwear, picked out by the glare of a hundred portholes, and shriek, 'Just GO to the bloody car deck, you morons. And someone tell that daft woman that asking her to page Mr C Lion is the oldest hoax in the book.' She can't hear, but it makes you feel better. Roll on the wild anchorages.

None the Wiser

It was somewhere in the Western Approaches that the thought hit. Do you know, we said to one another, counting on our fingers, it is over 20 years that we have been cruising together? Twenty years since the first bold venture in the Contessa 26 *Barnacle Goose* from Hamble to Ballinskelligs Bay: there, the log recalls, we saw three nuns paddling on the sandy beach with their skirts hitched up, spliced a rope strop on to the cockpit bucket (it lasted us for three boats before getting lost), and reluctantly gave up our ambition to sail out and land on Inishvickillaune.

Twenty years! Years in which we have raised children, had three beloved boats and one failure, and covered many thousand chilly sea-miles in our own boats from Belle Ile to Scapa Flow, Fastnet to IJmuiden. We have sailed round Britain and round Brittany (the inland leg taken via the Rance Canal, with the mast following on a lorry), and round Ireland. In charter boats we have sailed the Ionian and Aegean seas, coasted southern Turkey, and drifted on a warm Indian Ocean. Twenty years.

'And do you know what?' he said after a while. 'We haven't got any better.'

I considered this. Hell. He is quite right. Twenty years' cruising, and we cannot really, with hand on heart, say that we have improved.

I don't know why the thought occurred to us that we should have done; perhaps it is that we are encouraged, these days, to regard everything as progressive, and testable, and subject to measurement by exams and certificates. People are forever banging on at us about Lifelong Learning, and sailing schools call themselves a branch of adult education. If there are cruising grades we should by now have graduated from Day Dabblers to Competent Coasters to Offshore Officer-Class, or something. We should be on a permanent upward slope.

But who is, really? I suppose there are certain advantages to long service. We are rarely surprised these days by anything the weather does to us, and prepared for the wind to snub the forecasters, especially in the South Irish Sea.

We have a glum stamina about plugging on and on and on with nothing but greyness to look at. We are possessed of a certain low cunning when it comes to berthing, and have a probably unwise conviction that we can always tell whether the anchor has bitten just by feeling the chain and frowning. We have discovered by long and bitter experience that the navigator should never ask the tired, deranged helmsman 'Do you see a light flashing three?' but 'What is the light flashing?' Otherwise the deranged helmsman will answer 'Yes, three, oh yes, definitely,' while forcing himself to hallucinate a distant car headlight into a harbour mouth beacon.

But the rest? I dunno. Our navigation can't have got better, because there are now so many bleeping smug little gizmos down there that we have entirely forgotten how to Double the Angle on the Bow, and have got into the disgusting habit of punching the GPS button to check course, position and speed at the start of a watch before we even peer out on deck to get the feel of reality.

Our boathandling has to be re-learnt with every change of boat, and one of us at least – me – is generally lagging five years behind and can never remember which way she propwalks, or indeed what propwalking is, and therefore spends a lot of time with warps and fenders, on the foredeck, thus preventing the other crew member from making any progress at all at the art of untangling coils of rope in a hurry.

Then there is sail-handling and reefing and general deckhandiness. This might have got better with practice down the years, except that unfortunately we seem to get older and fatter with the passage of the said years, and the boats get slightly bigger, so we bumble around the 35-footer with much the same degree of incompetence and imbalance as when we first lurched on to the foredeck of a Jaguar 22.

The same goes for courage. As the boats have got stronger and

PEYTON

our experience wider, we have had children, and therefore got more neurotic about self-preservation, even when they are not on board. As for willingness to embark on long, wild passages, we got out of the habit of doing that with any enthusiasm during the Postman Pat phase, because of the horror of having bright, refreshed children waking up and demanding stories just when we had fallen into the pit after 42 hours at sea. Having discovered how easy it is to find night anchorages when you really want to, we somehow seem to day-sail a lot more than we did in the days when we were novices with everything to prove.

See? We haven't got better. We have possibly been on a very, very low plateau for 18 of the 20 or so years, and are starting to decline. It is time to push the curve upward again. Self-improvement!

Got one of those self-filling buckets with a bottom that flaps up? Good, eh? But have you done the thing where you want to pour something out of it carefully on board, so you put your other hand under the base to support it, and . . .

Flash, Bang . . . !

The trouble with cameras is that they cure fear. More than that in the hardened user, a camera creates a virtually total antidote to the instinct of self-preservation. Photographers walk towards guns and explosions, peacefully preoccupied with framing. I've seen them hang off roller-coasters, attempt close-ups of furious flying pickets and stroll, viewfinder pressed to the eye, in front of a hot-air balloonist's flamethrower. 'It would look really good,' said this last somnambulist lensman, 'coming right at the camera with the girl in her asbestos gear behind it!' Gently, his anorak began to steam.

The only time a flicker of self-interest appears is when the camera itself might be at risk. Then, they hunch a bit, but still try for that ultimate shot right up the trunk of the charging elephant.

It follows that photographers on boats are a bit of a liability. Frankly, as far as sailors are concerned the best situation is when the lensmen whiz up in fast RIBs steered by someone without a camera, and whiz away again. But it cannot always be so. Sometimes you have them on board. Sometimes, dammit, you are them. And, hand on heart, I can say that nearly all the truly heart-stopping moments I have ever had on boats have begun with somebody determined to take a photo.

There was the one who we nearly drowned, years ago when we had a Contessa 26. He wanted a really wide-angle shot of the cockpit from downwind . . . we got him back aboard just in time, soaked only from the waist down. Then he raced to the pulpit for a really interesting angle pointing up the deck as we fell off the next wave.

And there was the fellow who pushed himself off in the Avon without so much as a pair of oars, and began drifting towards the rocks, his motordrive whirring happily, returning our shrill cries of alarm with shouts of 'Lovely!' and 'Can you get that little brown sail at the front to bulge out a bit more?'

Specialist yacht photographers, of course, are a legend and know what they are doing vis-à-vis bulging sails and what might actually happen to someone with his leg hooked over the spreaders if the reef were shaken out. But even they are sometimes overtaken by the thrill of the chase.

I had a bizarre Channel crossing once on Rodney Pattisson's F27 folding trimaran, owing to some bet the great Olympian had made with *The Times* that he could sail from Studland Bay, Poole, to

Cherbourg, buy the ingredients of a gourmet picnic lunch and get back before the pubs shut.

The photographer, Sarah King, showed immense grit and speed in running after Rodney as he hared down the pontoon in Cherbourg with laden trolley, scattering baguettes in his wake.

On the way home, in perilously light airs (we eventually got back at dawn, actually) she became obsessed with the notion of taking a picture from the masthead – of the whole feast spread out lavishly on the cabin top. So we hauled her up, she got snapping and produced a great shot before the swell began to rise. Just as she remembered a dislike of heights, the feast started sliding to-and-fro, hurtling paté-pots into the spinnaker bags and tomatoes into the nets. We hardly knew which to save first.

Amateurs, however, are the least predictable of all. On one occasion, to celebrate the Royal Hospital School's new fleet of Shrimpers going on their first long weekend cruise, we sailed up the Stour to meet them with the headmaster and plenty of film. A fine sail, plenty of wind and sun; until the cameras came out nothing could be smoother. We rendezvoused with the little fleet of three and then the Head and I left the cockpit to the tender mercies of the skipper and son.

Inevitably, camera-frenzy came over us. In a freshening wind the crew chased the Shrimpers around, seeking ever groovier angles and closer encounters, while heedless of our safety, we slid around the foredeck and received violent clouts from the genoa track.

Click, snap, closer, lovely, yes, stand on, that's a super view of the bow wave, now why did you have to tack? What do you mean, collide? Looked miles away through my viewfinder. Oops, sorry! Was that your head? Didn't see it, was trying to get the lead boat just under the Harwich steeple. A fine day, flat water, a containable breeze, but still I have never come closer to sliding right under the guardwires and into the wet.

When I got my pictures back, there were some shots of a Sadler's hastily-reefed main without the slabs done up, featuring a brown blur in the background which might well have been a Shrimper. There were several bow waves, apparently shot through soup. There was a close-up of a Shrimper, marred by someone's bum as he tried to haul in his dinghy for prettiness' sake. There was an elbow, believed to be my own.

Home for Christmas

The boat is home! Home for Christmas. Perhaps we shall take her out a mince pie and a tumblerful of sherry, as we used to do to the late lamented Large Black pig in the orchard. Perhaps we shall put fairy lights round the pulpit to celebrate her first ever participation in the family festivities. It is strange, and rather wonderful, to see her here.

People with private docks, or water frontage, or broad river views-with-mooring, or a habit of fitting out 45ft ferro hulls in a sub-urban car-port, may raise an aristocratic eyebrow at my naive amazement. But for us it is still a giddy experience to look out of the bathroom window and see the Rummer home. There you are, yawning over the toothpaste at the usual blameless inland agricultural landscape, all damp, leafless trees and dead potato-tops and stout cart-horses and depressed-looking sheep – and in amongst them, like a queen, is a 35ft yawl with the barnacles still on her propeller blades.

Thanks to a debonair local firm with a lorry and a mobile mini-crane she now stands there, shored up casually next to the barn for all the world as if she expected someone to bring her a bucketful of minced-up mangel wurzels. Or, perhaps, milk her?

There was a tense confrontation the other day when Paul climbed aboard to pump a particularly heavy dose of rainwater out of the bilges, and looked up from the cockpit pump to see the three Suffolk Punches staring in wonderment over their gate. For days they had been looking with dim suspicion at the boat, plainly a larger animal than any of them, and wondering when she would show her true colours and start lumbering over on her wooden shorelegs to steal their hay. Now, just as they have decided the creature was not, after all, alive, it starts piddling! Later that day, being led past, each horse lowered its nose to sniff suspiciously at the damp patch left by this alarming new mutant species.

The reason for bringing the boat right home was partly economic. It cost roughly the same to have her carted up from Ipswich as it would have done to lay up in a boatyard, and if you lay up at a boatyard you always end up on the phone, having run out of time, pleading for certain jobs to be done before launching – a new anode here, a rudder bearing there, and oh God! the acres of exterior varnish. This happens even if you are competent to do it all yourself,

PEYTON

because whenever you drive to the boatyard it is cold, and starts raining, and the stove is dismantled so you can't make tea, and you have left the vital tool on the kitchen table anyway; so to hell with it, off to the teashop.

Well, this winter a lot of jobs needed to be done, most involving carpentry and rewiring. As it happens, I had the prescience to marry a fine carpenter and former stage electrician (not a lot of people know that my husband once personally rewired the Gents at the old Mermaid theatre). He finds that the desire to shape a new floorboard or install a tidier switch panel is stimulated by the sight of the boat, the proximity of his workbench, and the comforting knowledge that it is not far to the kitchen. For my part, there is an almost sinful sense of ease in being able to take every single thing off the boat and put it in the shed 20ft away without all the intervening business of trolleys, car boots, roof racks and evil temper. Not to mention the glorious prospect of loading up everything *including tinned food* at the beginning of the season, and letting the lorry take the strain. And the equally comforting thought that if the family economic situation takes a dive before the spring, we can keep the old girl right there by the barn, for nothing, until we can save up enough for another truck. We could always wait for a misty day and sit in the cockpit in our oilskins, playing recordings of sea sounds and pretending that the occasional puzzled 'moo!' close at hand is the Ile Vierge foghorn.

Or – it occurs to me with dreadful force on a wet, wild, windy, cold afternoon – if the economic situation looked up rather than down, we could wave a plastic card at the lorry driver and get him to round the Forelands, Dungeness, Beachy Head and Selsey for us, all in one afternoon and without benefit of tides. Or pop her up to Aberdeen for a quick passage to Bergen.

No, no, perish the thought. This is a cruising boat, not a trailer-sailer. We must round our own headlands. Mustn't we?

The Name Game

Put the order in at Earls Court, did you? Good feeling, eh? Be it an 8ft dinghy or a royal yacht, a boat is never so romantically adored as during days between commissioning and launching. We all know perfectly well that buying good second-hand boats is far more sensible, but you miss that virginal buzz. Nor, unless you are prepared to flout superstition and court bad luck, do you get to name the boat.

When I have written about boat names I have tapped into a vast unsuspected pool of emotion and controversy. The proposal was a simple crusade to get beautiful yachts given beautiful names, to save honest boats the disgrace of going around with things like *Attameeting* and *Passing Wind* written on their poor transoms. I expected a flood of letters from indignant owners who had named their boats *Costabomb* and *Askthewife* and could not see what business it was of mine to object. In the event, only one owner complained, and that was corporate.

But I did get a flood of letters. Some were from distraught second-hand buyers, torn between tempting superstition and keep a naff name; some of their plights were grave indeed. I suggested to the new owner of *Bonko Bonko Yum Yum* that he risk bad luck and change it. By the tone of his letter, I judged that otherwise he might become a serious danger to himself and nearby shipping the first time the coast radio called his name on the traffic list. You can't steer straight when you're weeping with shame.

Three people sent in either the name or the photograph of *The Bog's Dollocks*: one was an English teacher and co-owner of the splendidly named *Valkyrie*, who went further. Since all things are grist to a good teacher, in Conway Marina she compiled lists of

PEYTON

names, good and bad and odd alike, and fed this data to her A-Level students so they could investigate how people use semantics and language to project a desired image.

Little did the owners of *Puddy Maws, Kwik Decision* and *Masquerader* know that they were the subject of linguistic sociology; *Placid Princess, Whiplash* and *Chewsy* are now forever immortalised in academe. The students were psychologically subtle, working out that '-ie' endings (*Bonnie, Sheltie*) make a boat seem friendly, whereas full names (*Catherine Laird*) convey an air of class.

One essay pointed out that boat owners can choose between different tones to reflect their attitude to sailing: perhaps a lighthearted ring – *Rag Tag, Waka Tiki* – perhaps the tranquil effect of long vowel sounds – *Singing Wind, Sea of Dreams, Moody Blue*. It also pointed out that some see boats as social, and offer a deliberately 'hospitable' name such as *Sippinsherry III*. Another student sent a pie chart, quantifying the popularity of human names, sea words, wildlife, deviant spellings, romance and enchantment, music and dance, etc.

But then, twinkling across the Worldwide Web, came Jan Twardowski with news from the US seaboard. He and his wife, clearly the Hans and Lotte Hass of dreadful boat names, have collected for years. So take a deep breath and confront *Ecstasea, Whoopsea, Sea Esta, Sea-Ducer, Legasea, Seabattical* and *Playseabeau*. Then, moving on: *Spar Trek, Ferry Queen, Kantaforder,*

Blew-by-You, Out to Launch, and – presumably courtesy of a cheese spread magnate – *Dairy-Aire.* No, read it aloud. Ask your French friends, I'm not explaining.

I trust this list has been of no help whatever in inspiring anybody with a name for a spring launching. I would hate to think we had unleashed anything here that we couldn't control. Did I mention *Hava Kuki* and *Vitamin Sea?*

The Art of Kipping

The other day I was lying on an office carpet at Broadcasting House, head on a rolled-up jacket, staring up at trailing telephone wires and the underside of an office chair. I shifted my numb shoulders a little, and for the thousandth time heartily blessed the quirk of fate which led me to go boating while I was still young enough to acquire new habits.

The most valuable lessons in life, after all, tend to be things you never expected to learn. Officially, yachts are supposed to teach you all sorts of stuff which I have never quite mastered: independence and handiness and self-reliance. In fact, the most useful thing they have taught me is how to have a quick kip when I need it. Long before 'power-napping' was made voguish by American management gurus, I could doze for Britain. I am adept at losing consciousness on any surface and in the middle of any working day: all thanks to cruising. I go to sleep on trains with ease, head forward on the table. Driving long distances I pull into lay-bys and sleep for 20 minutes (or until a kindly patrol officer bangs on the windscreen). In my study I sink gracefully to the floor between paragraphs. Up at the BBC, if I finish a script early, I may well vanish head first under a desk, oblivious to the bits of fax paper which scatter over my supine body as in *Babes in the Wood.* Once, I arrived at a literary dinner so tired that I asked for 20 minutes in a quiet room 'to sort out my notes' and managed a fine nap with my face on a library blotter. One day I will do this so convincingly that the local Crime Writers' Appreciation Circle will panic and call out the police because they think somebody has been at me with a silver-handled paperknife.

True offshore sailors will recognise this catnapping tactic instantly. All I am doing is going off-watch: flopping down all-standing, boots and all, in the same way as you would in between sail changes on a wild night off Royal Sovereign. But without the conditioning of early

PEYTON

cruises, it would probably be impossible to behave like this.

There are people I know who can't sleep properly away from their own bed, even at night, and who get upset at the idea of falling asleep on a train full of strangers. To these normal people, unwarped by cruising, the idea of 20 minutes' oblivion on a strange office carpet would be shocking. So they soldier miserably on, yawning. But to the sailor a BBC floor is just the best bunk in the saloon: it's warm, it doesn't throw you around or drip in your face, and people don't keep trying to roll you aside so they can get their dry socks out of the underbunk locker.

I seem nearly always to have sailed shorthanded, even in the days when I was totally incompetent. So I know a bit about sleep deprivation in skippers. The classic moment came on my very first down-Channel trip, aboard an 18ft pocket cruiser in the middle of Lyme Bay on a foggy night. The wind was in the south-west, and since our navigational armoury consisted of one dodgy RDF, we were far from certain about weathering Start Point, or indeed where it was. But we knew we were in the middle of the bay somewhere.

At this stage the skipper, grey with fatigue after 20 hours awake, suddenly lost his marbles. We had already spooked ourselves by nearly hitting a surfacing submarine and setting fire to the floorboards with an overheating exhaust pipe. Now: 'This is it!' he cried dramatically, clinging to the cockpit coaming. 'This ship is now Fighting for her Life!'

I thought for a bit, pushing the tiller to and fro. I knew next to nothing, but I had slept all afternoon. He knew a lot, but was useless through fatigue. In the end I said: 'Tell you what. I'll sort of reach up and down for an hour or so while you go to sleep. We won't get far. This boat never does. There's no land close enough to hit. And if you get some sleep you might think of something.'

So he plunged into his bunk while I sailed aimlessly to and fro on more or less reciprocal courses in the fog. At 0400 he reappeared, once again Master under God, peered at the chart and came up with a brilliant scheme for feeling our way into an anchorage under Hope Nose. So we did.

The only difference between the despairing lunatic who went below and the born leader who came up was 40 minutes' sleep. I never forgot that lesson, and now – on sea or land – when in doubt I keel over sideways and get snoring.

Jack of All Trades

I ran away to sea, one summer. There we were in Lerwick, delivering our son to the last leg of the Tall Ships Race. And there was I stamping along the quaysides looking at all the jammy under-25s preparing to sail off to Denmark (youth is wasted on the young. What have they done to deserve it, eh?). Whereon I came upon the usual clutch of vast Norwegian square-riggers with the usual spare capacity, and that was that. After a brief doomed attempt to memorise the Norwegian for 'Fore T'gallant Buntline', I paid my money, fobbed off my various employers for a week and signed on to *Statsraad Lehmkuhl* of Bergen.

I shall no doubt return to this subject. You know how it is with midlife square-rig converts; the hammocks alone provide hours of reminiscence, and that is before the subject of futtock-shrouds comes up. But for now I will restrict myself to a meditation about small yachts, which developed during those long watches to Aalborg.

For the most striking thing about a big sailing ship is simply how many jobs there are. Even discounting the fact that you have to keep hordes of trainees busy, there are more different functions than had ever occurred to me. Even below officer level they proliferate.

The helm was one person, the lookout, for'ard by the bell, quite another. In between these jobs you scuttled around as a deckhand, galley hand, steward's assistant, bosun's gopher, or celebrant of a mysterious ritual called Firewatch, which involved touring every compartment in the ship four times in the hour and returning to inform the bridge that no sudden conflagrations had yet claimed the potato store, sail-locker, or gentlemen's lavatory, and that the freezer temperatures were correct.

Coming from a chronically shorthanded yachting life, I realised for the first time how many simultaneous functions we achieve all the time. When your spouse routs you out of your warm bunk in the middle of the night off the Longships and dives into his with a happy grunt, you instantly become not only officer of the watch, navigator, helmsman and lookout, but also the deckhand who trims the sails, the watch-leader who tells him how far to trim them, the bosun's mate who notices that the anchor is coming unlashed, and a host of other people.

If you want a cup of tea and a biscuit you are the steward; if you burn your finger getting it, or a child feels sick, guess who is the MO. When the fuel runs out in a long night's calm, you must call on your inner chief engineer to haul the jerrycans out of the stern locker. And all the time your eyes rove around in a visual version of fire-watch, checking that everything is OK on and below decks. Your only subordinate is an unintelligent self-steering device rather less fit to be left to its own devices than a 15-year-old seasick trainee, and a clock radio that is supposed to turn itself on for the Shipping Forecast and doesn't.

And perhaps you are the captain, too; or, in many couples, half-a-captain, meshing brains and wills with the other half in brief simultaneous periods of wakefulness to create a coherent policy for getting to some reachable port. And when you get there you become what Norwegians call the ship's sergeant, handling money and crew changes and matters of lowerdeck discipline involving the shaking out of bunks and swabbing of floors.

You manage somehow. You cut corners and compromise. Whereas on a big ship, with only one job at a time, you turn strangely perfectionist to compensate for allowing your other functions to atrophy.

I found the hardest thing was to be on the helm during a palpable, and favourable, windshift. You can report your views to the watch officer, but whereas on a yacht you would lean forward and goosewing the genoa, or try steering up 10 points to see how she goes, under orders on a big ship you have to keep on steering the old course, precise to a degree, until those above you decide to act on the wind-shift.

Likewise, a lookout may long to nip to the rigging with the rest during a manoeuvre, but mustn't, because for the moment his only job is to ting the bell portentously for every irrelevant smudge he sees on the horizon. Believe me, it feels weird. Like being a mother who is suddenly confined to nothing but nose-wiping, and only one nostril at that.

As the small yachts sailed up the Kattegat to meet us, looking divinely simple and bermudian after six days' clewing-up and bracing, the contrast was astounding. Because, after all, yachts are ships too, carrying the same responsibility in miniature.

The big-ship captain manages a complex workforce and addresses it once a day, by Tannoy, while the family yacht skipper manages only himself and whichever members of the family look most like co-operating. No wonder that in harbour we fall into such a deep exhausted sleep.

Until, of course, the Harbourmaster shouts that we have to change berth and pay up; and struggling from the fogs of sleep we realise that we are also harbour-watch, security guard, and accounts department of the shipping company.

There is something very restful about doing one job at a time. I might try more of it.

Crude Crew • 2

We have found the perfect crew and no, you can't have her address. Good cruising crew, like the philosopher's stone or the secret of perpetual motion, are the subject of endless questing. Adequate racing crews are no doubt reasonably easy to come by – if they make the boat go faster, never mind if you aren't soul mates; once you're out of the showers at the end of the day you can each find someone else to talk to.

But when you are cruising, you are – for the duration of the voyage – as good as married to the crew. You share a space with them not much bigger than a king-sized bed, all day and night. And there are moments when almost everybody needs them: sailors whose loved ones flatly refuse to come out on that horrible wet tippy thing ever again; habitual singlehanders or couples attempting longer

passages than usual, or (hardest pressed of all) young families needing to add another adult to the explosive multi-generation mix aboard.

The trouble is that competence on deck is not everything. After all, cruising is supposed to be a pleasure, and nothing spoils a pleasure like being mewed up in 10ft of cabin with someone who sighs a lot, or sniffs, or hums *Nearer my God to thee*, or tells golfing stories. On the other hand, one's best, dearest, most amusing shore friends can begin to pall when they've pulled through a few halyards (and then giggled), torn the clew out of the jib and trodden heavily on the hand-held GPS.

So you need competence, but not cockiness; reliability, maybe even a bit of experience, but not a constant debilitating challenge to the skipper's authority. This challenge, by the way, is not only verbal, 'Don't want to tread on your toes, old boy, but I think you'll find the inner passage flatter!' It is actually worse when it is unspoken. There are few things more demoralising than rushing up and down with kedges while some old sage sits at the helm, knocking the dottle out of his pipe and silently implying that he would never have been this close to the Soddit Sands himself on a Spring ebb, but didn't like to mention it.

The other thing is that the perfect crew must be available during the sailing season. If you are making a longer-than-usual passage (which is why you need them), that means quite a lot of the summer. Therefore, he or she must have loose or non-existent work and family ties.

Which leads to the question, why won't anybody marry him/her? And why can't he/she hold down a job? By and large, the tragic fact is that people who are competent are generally busy, and that people who are easy and pleasant to live with tend to have someone living with them, who objects to being deserted for weeks on end.

Nil desperandum: there are exceptions. There are students and gap-year takers and first-job kids with no money for holidays of their own choice (in this phase I crewed for a family with small restless children, thus developing valuable skills such as singing *The wheels on the bus* while reeving a topsail). There are the vigorous retired, whose spouse prefer golf or flower arranging, the newly redundant, having a fling; and the self-employed, who can organise their own time. Our new treasure crew is a freelance writer, perfectly happy to bring a fortnight's work with her and to keep in touch with her teenage daughters by mobile 'phone from somewhere off Erris Head.

Her work is not intrusive: all the way from Mizen Head to Oban she was reviewing audiobooks, which meant long periods on the helm with a Walkman, her lips moving occasionally and awful grimaces flitting across her face. It turned out that she was doing 'self-improvement' books, and found it odd to be in a tide-race in a rising gale with some woman droning on in her ear about making friends with your inner child.

Her domestic contribution was firmly to appoint herself 'Chocolate Officer and Nibbles bo'sun' and bring vast quantities of small, delicious treats to keep our spirits up. She regarded chopping vegetables as 'therapeutic'. In harbour she woke every morning at 0555, quite naturally, to write down the forecast then read peacefully till eight, when she served morning tea. At sea, her favourite watch was that foul one between 0400 and 0700, when you think you will see a beautiful dawn but it rains instead. Her perfections are innumerable: she is wiry and compact and tidy; she genuinely thinks that our quarterberths are quite comfortable, and she knows the words of songs.

And can she sail? Of course she can sail. Any fool can sail. It's the rest of it that's so difficult.

Movers and Shakers

A little while ago, we dismantled our life. Three weeks before Christmas it was all edited into boxes, from the relative sanity and neatness of 'L. VAT backfile' to the lurking horror implicit in the words 'kitchen drawers contents misc'.

And then there was the outdoor aspect of it. The new house is excellent but does not have attics or the sprawl of mouldering out-houses in which we used to hide our shame and chaos and shortage of time. Some autopsies should be done in secret, and I am too ashamed to say much about what we found in the capacious innards of the Boat Store. Some of it was more or less explicable (the out-board bracket from the last-dinghy-but-three, the shrimping nets used once) but some was downright humiliating. There was even a forgotten box of food: you know the sort of thing – bilge-ripened tins of steak-and-mushroom pie, best before 7.3.82.

But at least we had two months' warning and most of the work was under cover. It took me back to the strange interlude a few summers ago when we did roughly the same thing while tied up in a gale in Falmouth harbour. We had sold *Grace O'Malley*, our Cornish Crabber pilot cutter, in the middle of our summer cruise to a delighted German chap with long flowing hair, and bought the Rummer yawl. It was officially four feet longer on deck, but had the same beam; moreover, the new boat was not only finer and more graceful in her lines, but made of wood. All the same, she was not small.

Or not until, after a week's cruising, we tied *Grace* alongside her on transfer day and began decanting stuff so that we could cruise the new boat for the second week of the holiday. It was a wild bit of weather from the east, unleashing cloudbursts at the most inopportune moments. Heartily we told one another how good it was that we were not wasting a good cruising day. We began in high spirits, with the visible, rational, sensible contents of the boat: navigation gear, sleeping bags, clothes, lamps, torches, charts, all that.

Then – as the gale shrieked to its climax and around us halyards clattered and owners scuttled thankfully to the marina bar – we began on the deep stuff. As with the house-move, it was worse than psychoanalysis.

In a GRP boat, free from the ancient tyranny of rot, you don't always take everything off every winter. No, go on, admit it: you don't. We dived into the cavernous GRP stern lockers of our broad-bellied floating home, peered into the vast spaces beneath the quarterberths, and pulled out eerie objects fit for a nightmare version of *The Generation Game*: a sack of half-made baggywrinkle, circa 1987; a piece of Danbuoy; a baby lifejacket long outgrown; a plastic suitcase full of Duplo bricks forgotten after the round-Britain odyssey; the Irish Sea tidal atlas whose loss caused a memorable shouting-match off the Smalls lighthouse; the pelorus off the last main compass; a bag of WC spares from an SL400 we sold on the old Contessa when the first baby was on the way. How did that survive a change of boat, and a span of decades?

Well, you know how. Towards the end of a transfer, or house-move, or any packing, there comes a moment of pure panic. Things which hitherto have fallen into reasonably neat categories – Galley, Navigation, Bo'sunry, Comfort, Safety – suddenly become a mad irreducible minimum of objects you can neither understand nor classify, but can't throw away.

Partly it is puritan instinct which stops you chucking them, but mainly it is the confusion and emotional insecurity of what you are doing. So you stare for a moment, wild and confused, at the inexplicable thing in your hand. Reason is suspended, and you chuck it into a locker with a muttered 'Sort that out later'.

Only the new boat doesn't have those sort of lockers, does it? It has frames, and narrow V-shaped spaces where you want the air to circulate. So when we came to this emotional state we pushed the surplus objects into the car, which was a roomy estate with legroom when we began and a Mini when we finished at dusk. And eventually we drove the car home, and decanted that in turn. You've guessed where to: the Boat Store. And now, five years on, our sins are back to haunt us.

The Joy of Rope

Rope, don'tcha love it? I never can understand those prim people who only have two mooring lines and two springs in the cockpit locker. We have great coils and loops of the stuff in every length, type and degree of frayedness. It lurks up the foc'sle, sleeps in the lockers like a nest of pythons, and gets lashed in great lumps on the cabin top. And that is before you start going through the contents of two old sailbags in which we keep lashings in a dozen sizes, handy billies which might come in useful if ever we needed to lift a heavy weight (say, a dead sheep), assorted hairy tangles with snatchblocks spliced to them, and leftover sheets from the last boat but two.

We have speckled stuff and soft white stuff, evil mud-brown coils as stiff as uncooked pasta, and left over from the days when we rigged the GRP *Grace O'Malley* to be indistinguishable from a real old gaffer, enough of that unpleasantly prickly fake hemp stuff to set a public hangman up in business.

Can't throw any of it away. I have tried to make myself dispose humanely of a proportion of this writhing junk, but I always end up repreving each line, coiling it lovingly, and putting it back to bed in some shady nook, like a dear old dolly.

What Imelda Marcos was to shoes, I am to bits of rope. Not, of course, that the word 'rope' is ever heard on a sailing boat run according to tradition: except for the bell-rope (we have one of them, too), and I suppose the rope's end. Everything is correctly known by its function: halyard, sheet, stay, lashing, warp, painter, lanyard, downhaul, kicking strap, whatever. But the fact remains for any layman to see that we carry an inordinate and unjustifiable amount of what can only be described as old rope.

At the beginning of the season I try to cull everything that isn't attached to the rig. I start out with a reasonable allowance of functions: say, five mooring lines (bow, stem, two springs and a spare) and a long heavy warp for deep anchoring or towing. Then three or four useful 10m lengths of thin stuff for extending dinghy painters and other motley uses; and a spare set of jib sheets. In case. Oh yes, and two ready-made preventer lines with snapsnackles spliced to the end. And enough lashings for boathooks, broken hatches, dinghy oars and elastic waistband failures. Fine: there they all are, laid out nicely on the sidedeck, perfectly manageable, each with its own correct stowage.

Then I turn round and look at all the rest. The trouble is that every fathom holds a memory. It would be sacrilegious to discard the boom preventer from our very first Contessa 26: that's sailed thousands of miles with us and there is such a thing as gratitude. And you never know when you might need a spare pair of light spinnaker sheets, picked up for a song at a boat jumble at Framlingham Castle once. Never mind that the spinnaker is out of commission, due to large lacy holes all down one side. You never know.

And what about the stuff that was given to us by well-wishers? You can't throw presents away, or even hang them unwanted in the garage. There's the orange speckled stuff – lovely bit of line, that. Mountaineering rope, actually, given to us by our friend Dick when he thankfully gave up trying to be a mountaineer after having to be lashed to the rock face before he dared let go the safety line to eat his sandwiches. It is excessively stretchy, which rather reduces its usefulness, except as a very, very long anchor line, but we are fond of it.

Equally fond of the beautiful multiplait, far too long for most uses but too good to cut, which someone gave us when their uncle died. I think. It was a very long time ago. Then there's the very faded, very thin blue plaited line which has something to do with the sailing inflatable we used to have. It would do for tying up a burglar, perhaps, or lashing oneself to the helm, or towing a particularly smelly cheese a long way astern in a plastic box. You never know. I coil it up like a much-loved pet python and slip it surreptitiously in the sailbag when nobody is looking. Anything rather than get rid of it.

A boat's stock of line is her subconscious, her buried memory, her mysterious ID. Maybe what we need is a therapist.

The Wooden Way

Let us speak of gangplanks. We did a bit of gangplank sailing one summer: stern-to along the Adriatic. Afterwards I went on and on about this for many months: show any soggy Brit yachting family a bit of warm clear water with no tides and cheap wine, and we get over-excited and entertain sneaking thoughts of disloyalty towards our native mud.

But in these paradises, the one thing we do miss is the sheer idiosyncrasy of home boats. In a damp British harbour you have the great sport of deducing owners' characters from the look of their yacht. Look at that chap – raspberry-netting all the way to the cockpit, huge architectural sprayhood, massive pushpit. He wants a wheelhouse really, but his pride won't let him. Not when the boat is next to a 1930s number with raked mast, huge flat counter and no guardrails. And look at that crazy old Corribee, putting on racing airs with decal demon eyes each side of the bow; and the splendid old ketch with the Britannia Blue seams and a companionway as deep and dark as Tutankhamen's tomb.

And wow – quick, look, have you *seen* what's draped over the boom of *Fair Maid of Maidenhead* – black silk-effect double duvet covers . . . but her anchor's still in the maker's bubblewrap . . .

Many a happy half-hour can be spent in your own cockpit with a drink, eyeing-up the other boats. You start to see how fashion journalists get all that copy out of mere clothes.

In the Caribbean there is a different kind of boatwatching as you admire the workmanlike, scruffy appearance of the blue water liveaboards, with their ragged bundles of well-worn oars, patched dodgers and rust streaks on the hull. But in the Med, amid flotillas and timeshares, there is less variety. A whole row of sugarscoop sterns and a forest of biminis, gives you far less to go on.

Even the privately-owned yachts take on a certain bleached sameness: they do not welcome homely clutter, and make only bland statements like: 'I am reasonably rich.'

So we focused on the one aspect of the Medboat which does betray personality: the Plank. New charterers from the Northern world of finger pontoons blink with surprise when they discover that they are expected to teeter along a plain bit of wood balanced between stern and quay. Some even leave the sacred Plank behind when they set out, only to discover – after the first night's wild ritual dance with anchor, shoreline and Harbourmaster – that the missing lump of two-by-six is actually more important than all the in-mast furling and electric windlasses. It is their umbilical link with terra firma.

So we sat in harbours and admired other people's planks. Some, like ours, were functional lumps of wood with a lanyard on one end and the word 'SUNSAIL' fiercely hacked into them by some long-suffering fleet manager tired of tramping the local wood yards for replacements. I can report that ours was a fine timber, to which you would happily entrust the stoutest of skippers with the heaviest bag of provisions.

A local charter company, we noticed, gave its punters planks a full inch narrower and considerably springier than ours, thus providing hours of entertainment as nervous charterers reached the middle, dipped, started worrying, and stood wobbling on the bouncy beam, unsure whether to try walking backwards to safety or just lunge wildly for the pushpit.

Private yachts show more variety. Some have gaily-painted planks, with carved crescents to stow against stanchions on the side-deck; there are feckless cracked old floorboards that you wouldn't send a flyweight over, and lavishly-oiled teak numbers with anti-slip battens screwed down and the holes dowelled-in.

But the best one was up the peaceful Krka river. Tied up in

Skradin, we watched the arrival of a cavernous great Bénéteau, and gazed entranced while the skipper – an Austrian of advanced age and tortoise features – solemnly installed a beautiful wide aluminium gangplank complete with wheels and articulated shore step. He then made the two-foot transit over open water even safer by installing a full set of stanchions with guardwires neatly threaded through them. Then he put down a rubber mat to protect the unwary from tripping over the half-inch rise of the shoreward end. You could have piped the Queen Mum up it, with considerable pride.

The exercise took half an hour, and became precarious when Methuselah had to stand right on the edge to install his guardwires. At the end he called below. His wife, a third of his age, emerged in white strappy sandals with a roguish kitten heel, her bouffant blonde hair dyed to a hellish brilliance. She tripped across the cockpit, traversed the magnificent passerelle (flash word for gangplank) and vanished towards the showers. The skipper watched her with doting fondness. I turned to my own spouse to say: 'Some men know how to treat a woman!' But he had clearly guessed what was coming and had, mysteriously, vanished.

Hell on High Water

Every now and then, weary television schedulers commission a programme about Neighbours from Hell. Noisy ones, smelly ones, barbecue maniacs, encroaching swine who move fences in the night, and we all have a jolly good laugh, don't we, at how disastrously other people run their lives.

The sad thing – for those who enjoy such miserable entertainment – is that yachting is still regarded as an élitist toff pursuit, which therefore cannot possibly be typical. Yet you will never find such an agonisingly intense microcosm of neighbourly misbehaviour as you do on a long, fraying, Bank Holiday trot of small boats in a popular harbour. You can tell everything about a chap's character, social attitudes, nationality and emotional balance simply by tying up alongside him (or her – or, preferably, both together, in which case you also get a fascinating snapshot of a marriage). It begins before you even get close. Who could truly grow fond of anybody who hangs on his rail, on a busy weekend at a public quay, a neatly painted, insultingly premeditated sign saying No Mooring Alongside? What red-blooded Briton is not tempted to hurl it in the dock?

Even without the sign, some are able to make the depths of anti-social hatred in their hearts clear by sheer body language. Think how much venom can be injected into the deceptively simple act of taking a rope, passing it through a fairlead and handing it back. It should be made into a compulsory exercise for actors planning to do Hannibal Lecter.

Conversely, some of us decide to play it as Mr Cheeryble, disguising our dismay and rage at being trapped by a Fisherful of shrieking toddlers or a Westerly obviously weighed down by lager crates. 'There we go!' we cry, tossing them back their line. 'Have a good trip?' Then, with only an infinitesimal pause to let our fraudulent goodwill sink in, 'Want a hand with your shorelines?'

Then they haven't got any long enough, so you lend them a pair, and Mr Cheeryble mutates into Fagin in the night hours, peering out suspiciously every 20 minutes in case they sail away with his precious multiplait. Meanwhile, the camera could pan to the racy 40-footer inside both of them, whose skipper earlier announced that he would be leaving on the 0530 tide. This bluff – designed only to fend off neighbours – lands him with an agonising dilemma over whether to sleep in and lose face, or set out into the teeth of a northeasterly Force 6, in which case his wife will never speak to him again.

Eventually our camera catches him sneaking out at dawn and tying up to the fuel jetty ten metres away because he knows for a fact that there is no risk of it opening until ten.

And we haven't even started on the noise problem. In this age of specialised housing and homogenous neighbourhoods (yuppieland flats, suburbia, dormitory villages), boats bring unfamiliar kinds of neighbour. Everyone has different views about noise. The dawn chorus of toddlers is an unspeakable torture to the hungover bachelor; drunken midnight thuds on the foredeck enrage the weary parent.

Being British, we bottle up our fury so that after three days of being galebound the emotional maelstrom within each boat raises the noise level still further.

But maybe it wouldn't be such good television after all, because we are just too hoodwinked by the brotherhood of the sea to get truly nasty.

We once spent several days in Lerwick, wedged inside a pathologically sociable local boat. Owing to the midnight sun, true Shetlanders quite often don't go to bed at all in high summer, saving their sleep hours for the winter. Until 0400 nightly processions of friends and family scampered across our deck to the sing-song: you know, 'Hi ho, silver lining', starting up for the fourth time since the late shipping forecast.

In the end, we got strangely fond of the rolling party. The following summer, Paul rang me in a rather forlorn voice from the same quay.

'It's ever so quiet', he said plaintively. 'Spooky. I don't know whether I can sleep without the guitar man.' Luckily, someone then came down to the quay and told him that the Bergen–Shetland race was due in any minute.

Norwegians sleep even less than Shetlanders in summer: I thought that in the background I could just about make out distant, echoing cries of 'Skoal!'

A Word on Urea

In Boston, USA, during the magnificent progress of the Tall Ships race, the local organisers made themselves deeply unpopular by a cavalier attitude to berthing the gallant Class C entrants. Apart from shoving them miles away from the glittering squareriggers, and the trade stands, and the bars, they had some curious ideas about hospitality. *Ocean Spirit of Moray*, the Gordonstoun boat, ended up fastened miserably outside a rubble barge and was not one whit pleased to have sailed four thousand miles just for that. Never mind. Everything was much, much nicer in Halifax, Nova Scotia, when we all moved up the coast. The odds are that, one day, some of the young school crew who scrambled miserably ashore across that builders' junk will be running international business empires, and they will know just what to say when the Boston office asks them for a favour. Imagine it: the year 2030, and respectful minions marvelling as some unforgiving British tycoon suddenly snaps into his speakerphone 'Tell Winona P. Hackensacker that I'm giving the global conference to the Toronto branch. Why? I'll tell ya why! Because when I was 16, a load of Bostonians made me climb over a pile of rubble and walk half a mile for a shower, and I got back dirtier than I went.'

But, seeing the worst few berths set up a convivial train of conversation between us international escaped yachties as we spent the next week sailing up through the fog to Halifax as baffled supernumaries on the Russian ship *Mir*. Discussing the depressing time the smaller ships were given in Boston, we vied with one another to

relate the least attractive things we had ever personally tied up to. Naturally, everyone began by piously observing that when the weather is really bad you are just grateful to be in port, but after that the gloves were off and the hideous reminiscences came thick and fast.

There was a Dutchman who once spent two nights trapped in his botter in a defective lock, next to a barge full of sewage sludge. The worst bit was that the lock water was low, so not even a breeze disturbed the fetid air.

Then a Canadian said, with modest pride, that he had once tied up to an Icelandic trawler which he offended in some way, so that the crew threw fish-guts all over his deck while he was asleep. This led to many stirring reminiscences of sewage outfalls poised over forehatches, and to my story of coming out on the deck of *Grace O' Malley*, at Wells-next-the-Sea, to find every inch of deck and rigging covered in fine, clinging white powder – soya meal from the cargo ship alongside. Since all the ropes were already extremely fishy from the East Coast ports, we could have boiled them up and made a fine nourishing stew.

'But, soya is fine' said a hitherto silent figure in a mouldy canvas smock. 'Soya is OK. You wait till you get cat litter from a bulk carrier, spilt over you by the grabber, like I did in Glasson Dock one time. When it rains, it expands, right? As if it was soaking up cat's piss. And it expands in all the edges of the hatches and down in the cockpit drains, so they're blocked'. Another Canadian snorted and said, his voice dark with unspeakable meaning, that it was a lot worse if someone spilt powdered urea on your deck, because then the next wave that came over 'might as well BE cat piss'.

We all contemplated this in alarmed silence, and decided that tying up to rubble barges and fishing boats was OK, after all. Sometimes, kind fishermen even chuck a free cod or halibut on your deck. Sometimes they even miss your head with the bag of crushed ice they thoughtfully follow it with.

Even so, fishing boats may bring unwanted excitements. I met an elderly sailing lady once who recalled having tied up, with her husband, to a moored French fishing boat in L'Abervrac'h late one night. They used it as a pontoon with its full consent, but she was woken in the morning by loud engine sounds, choppy motion, and an unnerving illusion of being under way.

Emerging from her bunk (the husband slept very soundly) she found that it was no illusion. What with the fog and the hangover and the very early start, the French fishing crew had entirely forgotten its 26ft appendage and steamed out to sea. 'I have never, since that day,' said this woman darkly, 'undressed on a boat.'

All the same, real harbours are a lot more interesting than marinas, don't you think?

Aladdin's Cabin

We were hobbling over an Alp on our latest leisure discovery, hired snowshoes, when the beautiful thought came to my husband, Paul. The modern snowshoe, you should know, is a great improvement on the old, wicker, tennis-racket affair. It has sharp teeth to stop you slithering, lightweight steel-and-nylon webbing, and big holes to save you lifting chunks of powder with your feet.

We were enjoying them greatly, and brooding as usual on the possibilities of sailing north to the pack-ice one day, when Paul said: 'A pair of these hanging in your fo'c'sle and you'd be one-up on anybody.'

Silently, we both contemplated this vision. There you are, stuck in Brighton Marina with a net round the prop, or hiding from a gale forecast in Salcombe, and a casually-met fellow sailor comes aboard for a drink. After the usual polite exchanges about your elegant overhangs and tumblehome and respectful enquiries about GPS interfaces, or the practicality of a charcoal Pansy stove, your guest asks if he might be allowed to 'have a look around'.

Poking his head into the fo'c'sle, what does he see but a curious pair of giant, black, steel-and-nylon kippers, hanging neatly on a hook next to the spare warps.

'Oh,' you say airily. 'Snowshoes, yes, we do find them quite handy in the high latitudes, now and then.'

Glancing around, he then spots the windscoop and folded bimini, for low latitudes, a collapsible mountain-bike, the skis, harpoon, lobster pot, folding windsurfer, scuba kit and casually rolled-up set of flags labelled 'Gabon, Arab Emirates, Kerguelen . . .'

Impressed is not the word: the humble guest realises that he is dealing with a serious, world-travelling yacht, and therefore must refrain from drawing any wounding conclusions from the fact that you have been tied up for so long now that you have your own pewter tankard at the local pub and will be put on the region's electoral register any day now.

For me, there is always something strangely beguiling about a yacht that carries the paraphernalia of other pursuits. Who wants a stripped-out, purposeful, anorakish racing-machine? Who wants a boat with no reading matter on board, except the racing rules and a chewed copy of something called *You Too Can Have The Will To Win* with the cover ripped off to save weight?

Even the sight of a cruising yacht bookshelf containing nothing but books about sailing suggests a single-issue fanatic, rather than the more dashing figure of a rounded, gentlemanly, Edwardian dilettante.

Is it not much more comforting to see a chessboard lashed to the bulkhead? Or an embroidery frame thrust casually into a ditty-bag? Or a guitar and squeezebox hanging on special brackets (we have a customised whistle-holder for B, C and D penny whistles), a sketch of Table Mountain or even a half-finished sonnet sequence in a marbled notebook lying around on the chart table? At the very least these things suggest an owner who feels as much at home ashore as afloat.

Meanwhile, the folding bike (or, indeed, motorbike), walking boots and a row of pocket dictionaries assure you that this crew does not just arrive in a new harbour in order to sit, hunched on the cabin-top, scoffing Pot Noodles and impatient to set off for home on the next tide. These are people who explore, appreciate and savour new horizons.

I once heard of an American yacht with a neat, collapsible auto-giro flying device stored in the stern locker, for buzzing around new anchorages. Maybe we can't all manage that, but an inflatable canoe (for when the channel's too narrow for the Avon) might impress.

Especially if you also have a shotgun in a locked bracket in the corner with a tin box labelled: 'stun darts, crocodile/hippo only'. A few random bits of African statuary and oriental brass poking from corners of the galley shelves add character and a sense of adventure, although a stuffed penguin would be, I think, carrying things a little far.

I did see an old Thames barge once with a potter's wheel set up forward, and plenty of boats have carried a set of carving tools for the long, boring nights anchored up Norway's fjords. I have seen a sailmaker's sewing machine carried on long-term liveaboards, but think how much more sophisticated you would seem if, when visitors came down the companionway, it was not a mere hatch-cover you were hemming, but a tulle ballgown run up in mid-Atlantic – just in case you should dock in Hamilton, Bermuda just in time for an invitation to the Governor's Ball.

And if, by some oversight, they don't invite you, who cares? You have, after all, had the foresight to stow a solar-powered karaoke machine in a neat plastic box under the starboard berth, so you can make your own entertainment.

A boat is for life, not just for passagemaking. Go on, live a bit, fill it with diversions. Anything at all, as long as it isn't a telly.

Envoi, 2000 AD

Time for the Annual General Meeting with myself, and review of the sailing year. So here goes. As far as our own boat is concerned, let it be admitted that my part in the Great Arctic Attempt was small.

I crewed homeward from Stavanger to Woodbridge very slowly, eating mysterious things from Norwegian tins labelled *sodd* and *bog* and *snott* and *kakbols in brun sos* – many of which may have been cat food, for we provisioned in rather a hurry.

On the other hand, I had a fine time with the big ships; during Tall Ships 2000 I became a groupie, both in person and by website. This race, from Southampton and Genoa to Cadiz, Bermuda, Boston, Halifax and Amsterdam, was a fabulous enterprise. Particularly when you consider that the Cutty Sark race went on as usual in the Baltic, and that neither of them felt short of entrants.

The growth of the international tall ships movement, spearheaded by our own dear ISTA and fuelled by the quixotic efforts of many nations, is a marvel of the age. Fifty years after the last commercial grain-ships were pensioned off, the planet can still drum up a fantastic fleet: much of it under square sails. At a tall ships event you may see *Kruzhenstern, Mir* and *Sedov, Juan Sebastian de Elcano, Amerigo Vespucci, Cuahtemoc, Jean de la Lune, Europa, Eye of the Wind, Lord Nelson, Khersones, Royalist, Christian Radich, Alexander von Humboldt, Gorch Fock, Dar Mlodziezy, Danmark, Swan van Makkum, Georg Stage* . . . the list goes on. There are more, plus the gaffers and the modern fleet.

From *Jolie Brise* to *Maiden*, they become old friends as you wander the quays enthralled. They all hail from the land of youth; the rule that 50 per cent or more of every crew must be between 15 and 25 is unshakeable, so at the heart of the races is the passing on of a taste for sail and effort to a generation used to charter flights and Sony Playstations.

The combination of youth, excitement, apprehension, beer tents and language barriers adds to the surreal atmosphere in port, and enhances the sense of relief and clean purpose when at last you put out to sea. I got the taste for this at Lerwick, running away to Denmark on the *Statsraad Lehmkuhl*, and have burbled incessantly of hammocks and futtock-shrouds ever since. So the following year I waved them off wistfully at Southampton, took a bucket-shop flight to Seville and a train to Cadiz to wave hello again and watch them streaming over the Atlantic start-line.

Except poor *Mir* – on the guard-ship I stood with the great Captain Viktor Antonov, whose ship was delayed by a fault. 'I have never watched the start before,' he said, with a mixture of awe and regret. Later he set out, made up position astonishingly in the race, and the next time we met I was sailing on mighty *Mir* myself from Boston to Halifax, Nova Scotia. We took line honours, storming over the finish after five days and then bracing in sharp to hammer 40 miles out to sea overnight in a gale, because Viktor Antonov never sneaks into a comfy port overnight if there is a parade of sail to be led in the morning.

Then, having decanted my son on to *Europa* for his transat, I came home and followed the website. Actually, that had its rewards too. I clucked over them all like a mother hen: over the Polish trainee invalided off after a fall, with a doctor transferred at sea from *Kruzhenstern*; over the early gale and the dismasting of poor *Arung Samudera*; when Halifax stood by with a new-felled tree for her on the quay.

Captain Lt Sugeng Suryanto posted a message thanking the 'new horizons of the future about young people, the sea, tall ships and especially about seaman brotherhood. Good luck to all of you. We know the world is very small. We are sure we will meet again'.

Inspired, I booked on the only adult voyage of the summer, on the STA's new brig *Stavros S Niarchos*. Instead of meeting our son in Amsterdam by ferry, I contrived to join the parade of sail standing on a high footrope next to an extrovert 72-year-old Scotsman singing 'Flower of Scotland'.

Here the two tall ship race fleets of the millennium year met at last, on 17 miles of canal jam-packed with ecstatic spectator boats, from yachts to canal-buses, novelty canoes to stately barges. They all came together in stunning good humour, with hooting and jazz bands and national anthems and drummers, to welcome the great ships in from the sea.

It was extraordinary. It was Olympian. It was millennial. I have to admit that my husband Paul is slightly baffled by this sudden out-break of menopausal mastclimbing. But I'm with Lt Suryanto: long live seaman brotherhood, and we shall meet again!